Presented to:

_____

From:

_____

Date:

_____

*The future that we study and plan for*
## begins today.
Chester O. Fischer

# Hello Future!

*Insights for the Graduate*

## A GUIDE

## TO FULFILLING

## YOUR DREAMS

HOWARD BOOKS

A DIVISION OF SIMON & SCHUSTER

New York    London    Toronto    Sydney

**Our purpose at Howard Books is to:**
- *Increase faith in the hearts of growing Christians*
- *Inspire holiness in the lives of believers*
- *Instill hope in the hearts of struggling people everywhere*

**Because He's coming again!**

Published by Howard Books, a division of Simon & Schuster, Inc.
1230 Avenue of the Americas, New York, NY 10020
www.howardpublishing.com

*Hello Future! Insights for the Graduate: A Guide to Fulfilling Your Dreams*
Copyright © 2007 by Bordon Books

ISBN 10: 1-4165-3579-9; ISBN 13: 978-1-4165-3579-9
ISBN 10: 1-58229-669-3; ISBN 13: 978-1-58229-669-2

10 9 8 7 6 5 4 3 2 1

HOWARD colophon is a registered trademark of Simon & Schuster, Inc.

Manufactured in the United States of America

For information regarding special discounts for bulk purchases, please contact: Simon & Schuster Special Sales at 1-800-456-6798 or business@simonandschuster.com.

Product developed by Bordon Books, Tulsa, Oklahoma
Manuscript written and compiled by Rebecca Currington, Patricia Lutherbeck, and Noelle Roso in association with SnapdragonGroup[SM] Editorial Services
Cover design by Koechel Peterson & Associates

The quoted ideas expressed in this book (other than scripture verses) are not, in all cases, exact quotations, as some have been edited for clarity and brevity. In all cases, the author has attempted to maintain the speaker's original intent. In some cases, quoted material for this book was obtained from secondary sources, primarily print media. While every effort was made to ensure the accuracy of these sources, the accuracy cannot be guaranteed. For additions, deletions, corrections, or clarifications in future editions of this text, please contact the Publisher.

# INTRODUCTION

Your life is at a turning point, moving from one stage to the next. The excitement is palpable as you prepare for what is ahead—your future! No matter what direction your future takes, there are certain important truths, ageless bits of wisdom, and contributions from those who have gone on ahead that can be valuable to you on your journey.

*Hello Future!* is a book designed to place many of those principles in your hands. Why struggle when someone else has cleared the way before you? Why wonder when others have already gained insight?

We have filled the pages of this book with counsel and inspiration to help you fulfill your dreams, live your life to the fullest, cultivate your relationship with God, and finish your course with peace, joy, and no regrets. You will find profiles of champions who have forged the way, and stories of simple people who have tackled specific aspects of their journeys and succeeded. There are inspirational quotations and poetry, scriptures, and easy-to-follow instructions to help you along the way. We have included letters to you from God—based on what He has said to us in His Word, the Bible—and letters from others who desire to share important lessons learned.

We hope you will enjoy this book and refer to it often for counsel and inspiration.

*The Publisher*

# Contents

*Dream lofty dreams,*
*and as you dream, so shall*
*you become. Your*
*vision is the promise of*
*what you shall at last unveil.*

John Ruskin

# FULFILLING YOUR DREAMS

Using your God-given gifts
to be a difference maker and
discovering God's
unique destiny for you

# YOUR FUTURE IS NOW

The one thing you can say for sure about the future is that the possibilities are limitless. That's a wonderful truth—but it can also be a daunting one. Which path do you take? Which direction is right for you? Should you follow your mother or father's lead, that of an older friend or sibling? Perhaps you sense deep down inside that you are destined to be a pioneer, cutting an uncharted course through life.

Amazingly, some people already know—they've always known—what they are destined to become. For them the quest has always had a name and place in their hearts and heads. Most often these individuals' dreams are crystallized early in life by an unusually compelling motivational gift or a remarkable talent of some kind.

For most of us, however, finding our way into the future is a much more ambiguous process. The reality is we won't just awaken one morning and find it all mapped out in front of us. We won't have all the pieces to the puzzle at once. We find one piece, and that interlocks with another and another until a picture begins to form.

Your destiny is revealed and fulfilled one piece, one insight, one choice at a time. If you allow yourself to focus on the big box of 1,000 little pieces, you're apt to find yourself immobilized by anxiety, overwhelmed. Instead look for the pieces with straight edges—the pieces you need to define the boundaries. Some of those critical edge pieces have to do with your dreams, those holy imaginations that God has placed within your heart even as He was creating you.

It is **God** who works
in you to will and to act
## according to **his**
## good purpose.

Philippians 2:13

Each person has an ideal, a hope, a dream of some sort that represents his soul. In the long light of eternity, this seed of the future is all that matters! We must find the seed, no matter how small it is; we must give to it the warmth of love, the light of understanding, and the water of encouragement.

Colby Dorr Dam

HELLO FUTURE!

# IDENTIFYING YOUR DREAMS

It's simple enough for a child to say, "I want to be a fireman when I grow up." Astronaut, ballerina, movie star—children are big dreamers. But as we mature, somehow we lose the ability to visualize and verbalize our passions. Try this. Close your eyes and think back. What did you long to be as a child, even if just for a brief period of time? As these bygone thoughts come to mind, write them down in list form. There may be many or precious few just write what you remember.

Resist the urge to edit these "dreamlings" with your adult mind, and don't be concerned about practical applications at this point. This exercise is about identifying the childish precursors to your adult dreams.

## MY CHILDHOOD DREAMS WERE:

The next step is to write alongside each entry why that particular item interested you. Perhaps your favorite Uncle Sal was a fireman or your Aunt Betsy was a dancer. Maybe you felt a love for animals and dreamed of being a zookeeper, veterinarian, or animal handler. If you can, identify the motivation behind each one. Now draw a line through the ones that no longer interest you.

> By recording your dreams and goals
> on paper, you set in motion
> the process of becoming the
> person you most want to be.

Mark Victor Hansen

The next exercise is to create a new list. This time write down the items from your first list that are still of interest and add to the list more recent items that may come to mind, i.e., a speaker you heard in class, something you read about or observed on a trip.

Number these based on degree of interest.

This simple list (whether it has two items or twenty-two) is now the basis for both development and discovery. Carry it with you, and whenever you have a quiet moment, pray about the items on the list. Close your eyes and visualize yourself in those roles. Think about them before you go to sleep at night and ask God to inspire you as you dream while sleeping. Soon your daytime dreams will begin to coalesce and take shape.

HELLO FUTURE!

# We grow great by dreams. ... Dreamers see things in the soft haze of a spring day or in the red fire of a long winter's evening. Some of us let these great dreams die, but others *nourish and protect them;* nurse them through bad days till they bring them to the sunshine and light which comes always to those who sincerely hope that their dreams will come true.

Woodrow Wilson

Life has a way of slowly unfolding before us rather than stretching itself out in a panoramic view. That's because God has created us as free agents. Our lives are a reflection of our personal choices. Though He sees the end from the beginning and knows before we do where our choices will take us, He does not mandate them. Though He provides guidance and guidelines for our lives, He does not force us to observe them. Even the circumstances of your life—some expected and others unexpected—are subject to how you choose to respond.

Still, God has created you for a purpose—that's really what is meant by destiny—and He has given you certain gifts and talents designed to help you fulfill that purpose. He has also set dreams in your heart, dreams of what can be.

---

## Whatever you are by nature, keep to it; never desert your own line of talent. Be what nature intended you for, and you will succeed.

Sydney Smith

**HELLO FUTURE!**

## FACILITATING YOUR DREAMS

Now you're ready to test-drive your dreams on the open road. Caroline Jalango is a life coach for unstoppable individuals who are willing to step up to the plate and take a shot at living exceptional lives wherever they are. She offers these steps to achieving your goals and dreams in her article "7 Effective Ways to Set Your Goals in Motion Today":

**Stop seeking approval from people.** You don't need anyone's permission to fulfill your dream. Trust yourself and give yourself permission to succeed. Having support from people whose opinion you value is a wonderful thing, but it should not be the criterion for whether you begin acting on fulfilling your goals or not.

If you really desire to turn your dream into reality, constantly floating it around and seeking the approval of others will waste your time and kill your enthusiasm. What will happen if you don't get the approval of those whose permission you so desperately need? Nothing!

The future belongs to those who believe in the beauty of their dreams.

Eleanor Roosevelt

**Don't wait for perfection.** Waiting for a time when everything is perfect and in place will cause you to lose your enthusiasm and abandon your dream. Conditions may never be as perfect as you desire. You may never have all the money, time, or knowledge you desire to begin working toward your goals.

You must take risks, learn and improve as you go along, and then watch as everything begins to fall into place. If you have to wait for the perfect time to begin … you will be waiting a long time!

When you aim for perfection,
you discover it's a moving target.
George Fisher

A bird doesn't sing because it has an answer; it sings because it has a song.
Maya Angelou

*To fulfill a dream*, to be allowed to
sweat over lonely labor, to be given a
chance to create is the meat
and potatoes of life.

Bette Davis

**Create time for the goal.** Many people's dreams remain unfulfilled because they are too busy doing everything else except working toward their goals. If you are to accomplish your dream, you must be ready to invest your time and resources to ensure that it succeeds.

Making excuses about lacking the time is a procrastination tactic that will kill your dream before it has a chance to see the light of day. There is always time to work on what you love and consider important. Create that time and see your dream begin to unfold!

---

**The best way to make your dreams come true is to wake up.**

J. M. Power

**Decide once and for all!** The process of achieving your dream, like most things in life, begins with a decision. You decide what you want to achieve and then you plan how you intend to achieve it.

If accomplishing your dream is important to you, your inability to make crucial decisions about what you should do, how you should do it, and when you should do it will waste your time and impede your progress. Make up your mind and stop second-guessing yourself. When your mind is made up … nothing can stop you from making strides toward accomplishing your dream.

●

Until one is committed, there is hesitancy, the chance to draw back, always ineffectiveness. Concerning all acts of initiative and creation, there is one elementary truth the ignorance of which kills countless ideas and splendid plans: that **the moment one definitely commits oneself, then providence moves too.** All sorts of things occur to help one that would never otherwise have occurred. A whole stream of events issues from the decisions, raising in one's favor all manner of unforeseen incidents, meetings, and material assistance which no man could have dreamed would have come this way. I have learned a deep respect for one of Goethe's couplets: "Whatever you can do, or dream you can, begin it! **Boldness has genius, magic, and power in it."**

W. H. Murray

HELLO FUTURE!

**Be bold and take the initiative.** Be bold! You are the one in charge of turning your dreams into reality. You need to be proactive and enthusiastically involved in the process of working toward your goals to ensure you achieve them.

Just because you have shared your ideas with others does not necessarily mean you are no longer responsible for turning them into reality. Don't sit around waiting for others to make suggestions and guide your idea to reality. Don't leave your dream entirely in the hands of others. Nobody cares about your dream like you do.

You are never given a dream without also being given the power to make it true. *You may have to work for it, however.*

Richard Bach

# I will! I am! I can!

I will actualize my dream. I will press ahead. I will settle down and see it through. I will solve the problems. I will pay the price. I will never walk away from my dream until I see my dream walk away: Alert! Alive! Achieved!

Denis Waitley

●

**Invest in your dream.** No idea is self-funding. Don't be deceived into thinking that people will invest or finance your idea just because it is brilliant. Someone may choose to invest in it, but if not, you will have to invest your own time, energy, and finances toward activities that will fortify and fulfill your dream.

You may have to invest in the acquisition of knowledge or expertise that will help you achieve your goals. It would be a good idea to keep some money stashed away to finance your dream.

Go confidently in the direction of your dreams! **Live the life you've imagined.** Dreams are the touchstones of our character.

Henry David Thoreau

---

I could never convince the financiers that Disneyland was feasible because dreams offer too little collateral.

Walt Disney

**Do one thing at a time.** Commit yourself only to projects and activities that are connected to your main goal. Whatever you do should directly or indirectly add up to a move toward that goal. Failure to do this will confuse, overwhelm, sidetrack, and drain your energy.

To get started on achieving your dream, you need to plan for it and make it a priority. If you keep crowding and cluttering your life with what does not matter, you may never see your dream become reality.

Remember that you can't do all things, but you can do one thing![1]

*There are some people who live in a dream world, and there are some who face reality; and then there are those who turn one into the other.*

Douglas Everett

# The desires of the diligent are fully satisfied. Proverbs 13:4

# Hold Fast Your Dreams
### Louise Driscoll

Hold fast your dreams!
Within your heart
Keep one still, secret spot
Where dreams may go,
And, sheltered so,
May thrive and grow
Where doubt and fear are not.
O keep a place apart,
Within your heart,
For little dreams to go!

Think still of lovely things that are not true.
Let wish and magic work at will in you.
Be sometimes blind to sorrow. Make believe!
Forget the calm that lies
In disillusioned eyes.
Though we all know that we must die,
Yet you and I
May walk like gods and be
Even now at home in immortality.

We see so many ugly things—
Deceits and wrongs and quarrelings
We know, alas! We know
How quickly fade
The color in the west,
The bloom upon the flower,
The bloom upon the breast
And youth's blind hour.
Yet keep within your heart
A place apart
Where little dreams may go,
May thrive and grow.
Hold fast—hold fast your dreams!

# THE BEAUTY OF OUR DREAMS

Alison Simpson

When I was a little girl, I wanted to be a ballerina. I took ballet classes and practiced all the time. I listened to classical music and made up ballet routines. I owned a book by Margot Fonteyn and tried to emulate all her poses in my room. I really wanted to dance.

My parents knew this about me, and they willingly paid for ballet classes and all kinds of ballerina gear. My father was all about helping me discover my talent and my passion. In fact, as far back as I can remember, my father was always looking for that thing that created a spark in me. And he was always encouraging me to "do the thing you love."

But when I got a little older, reality won out when it came to my ballerina dream. The reality was, I just wasn't that graceful. And I certainly didn't have the lithe, fluid motions that it seemed I needed to have if I wanted to go further. And to be totally and completely honest, I just didn't really want to work at it anymore. So I stopped taking classes, put my Margot book on the shelf, and hung up my ballet shoes.

At about 9 years old, I started keeping a journal. It wasn't anything deep, just something that helped me work through challenges, thoughts about my life, and even just bad days. Soon, my writing included also poetry and short stories. And when I'd show my parents what I'd done, I could see it in their eyes … they thought it was good. Certainly not the work of a child prodigy, but it was good.

But even for all the writing I did, my parents were usually the only ones to see it. I didn't make a big deal out of it. In school I always got high marks for my writing. But I never wrote for accolades. I did it for me. Being a writer wasn't something that seemed realistic for my life. I guess I figured it was another ballerina dream. And by that time, I was really into music, and I figured that would be my career. In fact, I was convinced of it. This was my thing that my dad always talked about. I'd go to college and study music education, then get my certification in music therapy, and that would be my profession. It just made sense and I liked it. I even won a music scholarship to college and thought I was definitely on my way.

But no, that wasn't it either. I realized that during my sophomore year of college. I was sure that was not the direction for me. I declined my scholarship that year and changed my major to "undecided." I prayed, I studied all the different ways that God guides us, and I started searching myself—my dreams, my desires, what was realistic for me, and what was not. I found the answers in something that had long been like a best friend but not one I ever considered a realistic career—writing. I wrote a lot, that's for sure, but I never considered myself a writer.

So I declared myself a journalism major, and three years later, I had earned my degree. And to this day I'm still writing, and I'm getting paid to do it. And it's still something I'd do even if I never got a penny for it.

Dreams and aspirations are beautiful and valuable. They awaken our minds and encourage us to look beyond our present circumstances to what we could be. And while we may never achieve all that we could be, we are motivated to work harder when we value our dreams. I love my dreams because they help me understand myself and appreciate myself. I know I won't achieve them all. But I have achieved some of them, and I'm very proud of myself for that. I didn't do it through any kind of intrinsic talent alone. I did it because I worked hard and I wanted it bad enough.

Sometimes the dreams of young ballerinas and reality are two different things. But sometimes, they meld together with a very unique combined reaction that will astound you in ways you never imagined. Don't be afraid to dream, but don't be afraid of reality. If you're looking to God for direction and allowing yourself to dream and also to be lucid about your life, you'll be living a beautiful reality … which is much better than just a dream. [2]

# The moment of enlightenment is when a person's dreams of possibilities become images of probabilities.

Vic Braden

If you don't have a dream,
how are you going to
make a dream come true?

Oscar Hammerstein

---

## Dream big and dare to fail.

**Norman D. Vaughan**

---

Do you want to know what I most

regret about my youth? That I

didn't dream more boldly and

demand of myself more

impossible things.

Lewis Mumford

Some people dream in bright flourishes of color, dramatic themes played out in vivid detail, accompanied by haunting musical scores. Others dream in plain old black and white, low key, practical, no nonsense. Most of us fall somewhere in the middle, but we all dream—both in our sleep and in our waking hours—and our dreams keep us alive.

Roberta S. Culley

# YOU CAN DO THIS!

Brenna Fay Rhodes

I tried to hold back the tears, but it was no use. They snuck down my cheeks before I even made it into the kitchen.

Mom was standing at the window with her back to me, looking out. "Isn't it gorgeous today? My redbud tree is just one solid bloom and the amaryllis are stunning," she said. She turned toward me and her smile faded. "Hey, what's the matter? What is it, honey?"

I didn't even answer but handed the stack of mail to her and flopped down at the table. She read the open letter on top, then asked, "So, what's the problem?" She poured herself a cup of coffee and stood beside me.

My thoughts came out in a rush. "I just can't believe it, Mom. I worked my hardest. I paid for tutors, met with study groups. I studied constantly. I still failed. An F! I can't believe I have an F in calculus," I said.

Mom hugged me and said, "I'm sorry. That stinks to work so hard and not be successful. I'm really sorry." She handed me a tissue and sat down at the table.

I sniffed and blew my nose. "This is going to kill my grade point average. I'll lose my scholarships and probably never get another university grant. What if I lose my student internship?" I said. "Then I won't get the job I want, because no one is going to hire a complete failure. I'm not strong enough to keep working like this and still fail. It's just too hard. I'll never get over this. Never."

Mom handed me another tissue. She added cream to her coffee and stirred slowly as she spoke.

"Your Grandmother Feaster studied to be a teacher when no one believed in her or her dreams. No one helped her. The college administration didn't really want her there because she was a woman. Her parents thought she was crazy and refused to help her, so she paid her own way. Through hard work and determination she earned the respect of her professors. She was one of the first women in Texas to earn her college degree. She persevered and got her diploma, and she went on to influence the lives of hundreds of students during her long teaching career. When I was a little girl, I knew that I'd grow up and get my degree and be a teacher, just like my mother. I figured if she could achieve her dream with the whole world against her, surely I could, too. So I did." Mom straightened the blue placemat in front of her and smiled at me. "You come from tough stock, honey. You can do this."

I stared into space and pictured my grandmother as a young woman. In old photographs, she looks a lot like me.

Mom put her hand on top of mine and squeezed. "I guarantee you this: ten years from now, you won't even remember today," she said. "Life goes on, and what seems insurmountable today is really just a blip on the radar screen of your life. Go ahead and feel disappointed today. Then get over it. God has big plans for your life. Pick yourself up, dust yourself off, and get back in the game. You, my dear, are stronger than you think."

She was right, as mothers usually are. None of the disasters I predicted came true after that F on my grade report. I went on to graduate with honors and enjoy a fulfilling career. No one ever asks to see my calculus grade from college. I've experienced hundreds of days filled with incredible joy, and I've survived several days filled with tragic grief. Life is more complicated and sweeter and fuller now than I ever could have imagined that warm spring day at the kitchen table when I was a junior in college, staring at my first bad grade on university letterhead.

But Mom was wrong about one thing: more than ten years later, I do remember that day and that failing grade—with clarity. I will never forget that day. That's the day I realized my grandmother had paved the way for me to reach all my goals. She set an example of strength for me and for my children, and for their children. With my grandmother behind me and the Lord as my source, I am stronger than I imagined. [3] ⚡★

God often takes a course for accomplishing
His purposes directly contrary to what our
narrow views would prescribe.
He brings a death upon our feelings,
wishes, and prospects when He is about to
give us the desire of our hearts.

John Newton

# Dreamers and doers—

the world generally divides people into those two classifications, but the world is often wrong. Dreaming is just another name for thinking, planning, devising—another way of saying that a person exercises his soul. A steadfast soul, holding steadily to a dream ideal, plus a sturdy will determined to succeed in any venture, can make any dream come true. Use your mind and your will. They work together for you beautifully if you will give them a chance.

B. N. Mills

# MAXIMIZING YOUR TALENTS AND GIFTS

At this point, you may or may not know exactly what your innate talents and gifts are. For many those natural abilities reveal themselves early—the budding pianist or singer, the young person who seems to have a way with words, someone with a strong bent toward mechanics or organization. Still, you may not have clarity concerning which talents and gifts you want to pursue in the future. Ask yourself these questions:

**What gifts and talents am I aware of in my life?**
Most people can easily identify their gifts and talents. Begin by making a list of those you've already noted. Don't be shy! All talent is measured in degrees. A bit of talent is still talent. And don't forget about those that are less obvious: cooking, gardening, dealing with people, problem solving, etc.

> **The real tragedy of life is not in being limited to one talent, but in the failure to use the one talent.**
> Edgar W. Work

*We have different gifts, according to the*

*grace given us.*

Romans 12:6

⚙ **Am I using all my gifts and talents toward the fulfillment of my dream?** If your dream is to be a sculptor, it is simple enough to determine whether you have artistic talent—and that particular one. But in the bright light of your grandest talents, you may overlook others who have disappeared into the glare. For example, you may also be a talented people person or money manager. Don't hesitate to develop those talents as well. Even if you are supremely successful and your sculptures are lauded around the world, you will need to be able to properly manage the financial rewards of your work, and you will need to be able to manage the people who surround you because of your talent—art dealers, publicity people, schedulers, etc.

Many talented people overlook the fact that God gives us what we need to be successful. He will either give you personally all the talents you need to succeed as a sculptor, or He will bring someone into your life who possesses those support talents. Look for them; develop them; thank God for them.

Every one of us has a unique genius inside of us waiting to be revealed. If you **tap into your innate strengths and talents,** you'll find that you excel much easier in the world of work. The job market is tough now, and companies are offering fewer promotions, but there will always be opportunities for those who are recognized as having special talents and excelling at what they do.

Robin Ryan

### ⚙ Am I using my gifts and talents to contribute toward the fulfillment of someone else's dream?

Not everyone has a gift or talent that is destined for the spotlight. Your gifts may be designed to provide support for others. Every performer, for example, is surrounded by a number of people talented in their own right—designers, managers, public relations professionals, musicians, etc. Your gifts may be of this nature.

Resist the urge, for example, to sit on your singing talent because you aren't a Celine Dion or a Josh Groban. Become a backup singer or sing in your local church or community choir. As a talented mechanic, you might dream of working on the NASCAR circuit. Then again, you might dream of working with other mechanics for a local business owner. Dreams are not always about fame and fortune and the limelight. Most often they are about doing what you love to do in an environment that challenges you and brings you joy.

## Do not let what you cannot do interfere with what you can do.

John Wooden

HELLO FUTURE!

⚙ **Which of my natural talents must be developed in order to achieve my dream?** Have you ever put your dream down on paper? If not, it's time to do so. Quickly now—your future is waiting! On a large sheet of paper, draw a circle in the middle and write your dream in the center. Use fewer than ten words.

**My dream is to be an astronaut.**

Now from the circle draw straight lines out to the margin on the paper. On those lines write the various talents, skills, and educational requirements you will need to achieve your dream.

**Strong math skills**
**Physical fitness**
**Physical dexterity**
**Mechanical ability**
**Entrance into the NASA program for astronauts**

This process will help you decide if your dream is one that is consistent with your talents and skills. It will also give you a clearer picture of what goals must be achieved on the way. Many people make the mistake of thinking that the dream is the destination. Actually, reality is the destination, gazing out of the window of the international space station is the destination—your dream is the road you must travel to that reality. Sitting in the backyard staring at the night sky will certainly help you dream, but it won't help you ride your dream to reality.

Fortunate is the person
who has developed the self-
control to steer a straight course
toward his objective in life,
without being swayed from his
purpose by either commendation
or condemnation.

Napoleon Hill

HELLO FUTURE!

✵ What weaknesses do I need to overcome so that my talents can move me toward my dream? Equally as important as developing your gifts and talents is the need to evaluate your weaknesses. You may be a person with poor eyesight who desires to be a surgeon or an entrepreneur with procrastination issues. Making your dreams reality requires that you identify and overcome those weaknesses. For the surgeon, the answer might be laser eye surgery; for the entrepreneur, a class in time management. Weaknesses untended will bring you down, but weaknesses rightly appraised and dealt with will put your future on the road to success.

*Strengthen ye the weak hands,*
*and confirm the feeble knees.*

Isaiah 35:3 KJV

---

We should keep up in our hearts a constant sense of our own weakness, not with a design to discourage the mind and depress the spirit, but with a view to drive us out of ourselves in search of divine assistance.

**⚙ What opportunities can I think of to develop my talents?** It's possible to get so focused on the big picture—your dream to the max—that you fail to see opportunities when they are staring you right in the face. Your dream marketing job, for example, might be filling the picture in your mind so completely that you dismiss the ad soliciting individuals who would be interested in writing advertising copy on a contract basis for a small agency. No, it isn't the high-powered job you imagined, but it may serve as a good place to learn the realities of your local business community, gain exposure and experience, and make contacts. No one starts at the top.

Watch for those small, inconspicuous opportunities that could lead to something bigger, something better. When they come, snatch them up and work at them with the same determination and sense of mission that you would if that dream job were yours today. Your future is built with the bricks you make today.

●

*The heights by great men reached and kept,*
*Were not obtained by sudden flight*
*But they, while their companions slept,*
*Were toiling upward in the night.*

Henry Wadsworth Longfellow

HELLO FUTURE!

**Five minutes,** just before going to sleep, given to a bit of directed imagination regarding achievement possibilities of the morrow, will steadily and increasingly bear fruit, particularly if all ideas of difficulty, worry, or fear are resolutely ruled out and replaced by those of accomplishment and smiling courage.

Frederick Pierce

# THE PERFECT PLACE TO START

Coleen P. Kenny

"I'm going to be a pediatric nurse," I told my mom.

"I'm going to be a pediatric nurse," I told the guidance counselor.

"I'm going to be a pediatric nurse," I told the nursing professor.

I'd set my sights on nursing after receiving a Hasbro play nurse kit complete with plastic stethoscope and cardboard eye chart when I was six. I'm not sure when I chose the pediatric track—maybe while babysitting the munchkin next door.

Fifteen years later, the first clinical rotation in nursing school landed ten of us on a pediatric unit. *The perfect place to start!* I thought.

We arrived at 7:00 a.m. with real stethoscopes slung around the collars of our crisp white dresses (no caps, thank goodness), and we received our assignment for the day. After two years of liberal arts and textbook nursing classes, we were eager to get our hands on real live patients.

My imagination could not have conjured a day more different.

Nothing clicked. No bond formed with my tiny patient. No bond formed with the instructor who grew impatient with my lack of IV skills. I'd never set one up before. I was as miserable as a cat falling into a commode. I could not wait for those seven weeks to end. *What happened?* I thought. *Did I choose the wrong profession?*

The experience shoved my preconceived notions of pediatric nursing out the door and left me gun-shy of our next rotation: geriatrics. I've never been to a nursing home. I have no grandparents. I don't know any old people. If the kids I dreamed about didn't fulfill my plan, how could this turn out any better?

I arrived on the geriatric rehab unit with little enthusiasm. Finishing the semester and rethinking my major were my only goals.

A different instructor met us that sunny October morning. The third-floor nursing-station window framed a giant fireball of a maple tree, and the staff greeted us warmly. The unit didn't smell, and no one was moaning or tied down like in all the old movies.

We dispersed to our assigned rooms, and an elderly gentleman awaited this uncertain student. Mr. T, due to a stroke, needed help bathing and getting dressed, and he allowed me to practice making a bed with a full-size immobile man rather than the lightweight plastic mannequin from our practice lab. With the instructor's supervision, I administered his medications and took his blood pressure. The day moved as swiftly and smoothly as a ski on new snow, and I returned to my dorm without tears.

Excitement rather than dread accompanied the following Tuesday. The instructor assigned ninety-year-old Mr. T again, so I listened to report, then walked to his room, hoping to find out how his therapy was going.

Nothing could have prepared me for what I found. A slew of medical students and interns in long white coats surrounded Mr. T, fighting him to insert an IV and breathing tube. *What happened?*

*What are they doing to my patient? What changed in the thirty minutes since the night nurse handed off her charge?*

Mr. T's struggle broke my heart. Reality-shocked, I froze in the doorway.

As Mr. T jerked his head to evade the breathing tube, his eyes locked on mine. Fingers clenching a cold metal bed rail stretched toward me. I stepped forward, and he grasped my hand with amazing strength. Staring into my eyes, his body relaxed, and the clinicians were able to complete their stabilizing work. I sat with Mr. T until the ambulance transported him to the acute-care facility.

The instructor assigned me another patient, but Mr. T remained in my mind. As the seven weeks progressed, I not only stopped rethinking my major, I applied and worked as a nurse's aide on the unit for the final two years of school, and I was present when Mr. T passed away. When I received my bachelor's degree and passed the RN licensure exam, the unit became home for the first two years of my career.

Since then, I've been a head nurse in a nursing home, worked in home care, and after earning my master's degree and nurse practitioner certification, I have worked in long-term care for nine years and counting.

The elderly don't scare me anymore, and the gifts I receive on a daily basis from a profession I'd never even considered confirm my calling. Someone Else knew where I belonged and arranged the circumstances to get me here. So when new opportunities arise, I release my brain's preconceived notions and pray, *Show me.* And when people say, "How can you work with old people?" my reply is always the same: "How can I not?"[4] ⚡★

# A HANDFUL OF CLAY

Henry Van Dyke

There was a handful of clay in the bank of a river. It was only common clay, coarse and heavy; but it had high thoughts of its own value, and wonderful dreams of the great place which it was to fill in the world when the time came for its virtues to be discovered.

Overhead, in the spring sunshine, the trees whispered together of the glory which descended upon them when the delicate blossoms and leaves began to expand, and the forest glowed with fair, clear colors, as if the dust of thousands of rubies and emeralds were hanging in soft clouds above the earth.

The flowers, surprised with the joy of beauty, bent their heads to one another, as the wind caressed them, and said: "Sisters, how lovely you have become. You make the day bright."

The river, glad of new strength and rejoicing in the unison of all its waters, murmured to the shores in music, telling of its release from icy fetters, its swift flight from the snow-clad mountains, and the mighty work to which it was hurrying—the wheels of many mills to be turned, and great ships to be floated to the sea.

Waiting blindly in its bed, the clay comforted itself with lofty hopes. "My time will come," it said. "I was not made to be hidden forever. Glory and beauty and honour are coming to me in due season."

One day the clay felt itself taken from the place where it had waited so long. A flat blade of iron passed beneath it, lifted it, and tossed it into a cart with other lumps of clay, and it was carried far away, as it seemed, over a rough and stony road. But it was not afraid, nor discouraged, for it said to itself: "This is necessary. The path to glory is always rugged. Now I am on my way to play a great part in the world."

But the hard journey was nothing compared with the tribulation and distress that came after it. The clay was put into a trough and mixed and beaten and stirred and trampled. It seemed almost unbearable. But there was consolation in the thought that something very fine and noble was certainly coming out of all this trouble. The clay felt sure that, if it could only wait long enough, a wonderful reward was in store for it.

Then it was put upon a swiftly turning wheel and whirled around until it seemed as if it must fly into a thousand pieces. A strange power pressed it and molded it as it revolved, and through all the dizziness and pain it felt that it was taking a new form.

Then an unknown hand put it into an oven, and fires were kindled about it—fierce and penetrating—hotter than all the heats of summer that had ever brooded upon the bank of the river. But through it all, the clay held itself together and endured its trials, in the confidence of a great future. "Surely," it thought, "I am intended for something very splendid, since such pains are taken with me. Perhaps I am fashioned for the ornament of a temple, or a precious vase for the table of a king."

At last the baking was finished. The clay was taken from the furnace and set down upon a board, in the cool air, under the blue sky. The tribulation was passed. The reward was at hand.

Close beside the board there was a pool of water, not very deep, nor very clear, but calm enough to reflect, with impartial truth, every image that fell upon it. There, for the first time, as it was lifted from the board, the clay saw its new shape, the reward of all its patience and pain, the consummation of its hopes—a common flowerpot, straight and stiff, red and ugly. And then it felt that it was not destined for a king's house, nor for a palace of art, because it was made without glory or beauty or honor; and it murmured against the unknown maker, saying, "Why hast thou made me thus?"

Many days it passed in sullen discontent. Then it was filled with earth, and something—it knew not what—but something rough and brown and dead-looking was thrust into the middle of the earth and covered over. The clay rebelled at this new disgrace. "This is the worst of all that has happened to me, to be filled with dirt and rubbish. Surely I am a failure."

But presently it was set in a greenhouse, where the sunlight fell warm upon it, and water was sprinkled over it, and day by day as it waited, a change began to come to it. Something was stirring within it—a new hope. Still it was ignorant, and knew not what the new hope meant.

One day the clay was lifted again from its place and carried into a great church. Its dream was coming true after all. It had a fine part to play in the world. Glorious music flowed over it. It was surrounded with flowers. Still it could not understand. So it whispered to another vessel of clay, like itself, close beside it, "Why have they set me here? Why do all the people look toward us?" And the other vessel answered, "Do you not know? You are carrying a royal scepter of lilies. Their petals are white as snow, and the heart of them is like pure gold. The people look this way because the flower is the most wonderful in the world. And the root of it is in your heart."

Then the clay was content and silently thanked its maker, because, though an earthen vessel, it held so great a treasure.

Dear Friend:

Dreams are powerful. Throughout the ages, men and women have pursued their dreams, counting the struggle as nothing and pushing forward until in some cases they achieved results they could never have anticipated.

But some people invest their lives, their energy, in dreams that simply don't fit them. You've seen these unfortunate individuals on television, crying real tears of anguish, chained to a dream into which they have no talent to invest.

These misguided individuals are motivated by a number of things—love for the trappings of fame and fortune, a need to sabotage their personal success by choosing a venue where they cannot possibly succeed, a distorted self-image. Some have locked into the often-touted notion that they can be anything they choose to be. There is truth in that statement, but it is a reasonable truth. Some doors were never meant to be opened.

If God has placed a dream in your heart, then you can be sure your gifts and talents will coincide with that dream. He is fully committed to your success. He would never set you up to fail. That's why it's important to evaluate your dreams—give them a reality check. Ask God to help you identify and discard those dreams that are inconsistent with who He created you to be. Remember that pursuing and achieving the dream that He has placed in your heart will take your full concentration.

Your God-given dream won't necessarily be easy to achieve. You may even then be asked to overcome close-to-impossible odds, but your efforts will produce results rather than continual disappointment and frustration. In addition, you will have God as an ally, helping you along the way, strengthening your resolve, and providing opportunities.

Don't waste your time with dreams that aren't worthy of the person God made you. Your future is too important.

Best wishes,

*Roberta*

## The truth of the matter is that there's nothing you can't accomplish if:

1. You clearly decide what it is that you're absolutely committed to achieving.
2. You're willing to take massive action.
3. You notice what's working or not.
4. You continue to change your approach until you achieve what you want, using whatever life gives you along the way.

Anthony Robbins

*The weakest among us has a gift,*
*however seemingly trivial,*
*which is peculiar to him and which worthily*
*used will be a gift also to his race.*

John Ruskin

He who wishes to fulfill his mission in the world must be a person of one idea, that is, of one great overmastering purpose, overshadowing all his aims, and guiding and controlling his entire life.

Charles Bate

HELLO FUTURE!

No dreamer is ever too small;
no dream is ever too big.

Author Unknown

---

If your dreams turn to dust,
vacuum.

Author Unknown

---

In dreams and in love there are
no impossibilities.

Janos Arany

*Hold fast to dreams,* for if dreams die,
*life is like a broken winged bird that cannot fly.*

Robert Frost

*Most people never run far enough on their first
wind to find out they've got a second.* **Give
your dreams all you've got,** *and you'll be
amazed at the energy that comes out of you.*

William James

**Reach high,** *for stars
lie hidden in your soul.*
**Dream deep,** *for every dream
precedes the goal.*

Pamela Starr

HELLO FUTURE!

I have learned at least this by my experiments: that if one advances confidently in the direction of his dreams and endeavors to live the life which he has imagined, he will meet with a success unexpected in common hours.

Henry David Thoreau

# FOR THE LOVE OF GOATS

Kimberly J. Fish

Kali Cavanaugh patted Queenie's brown hindquarters as the goat climbed up the shallow steps and through the window frame following a short line of other milking goats ambling toward the pasture. Dusting her hands, Kali leaned through the sill reaching for the glass-paned window, but her nose caught scents of rosemary and lemongrass weaving through the currents in the air. As Joaquin poured Queenie's gallon-and-a-half offering into the pasteurizer, Kali walked around the milking station, ducking her head under the large wooden beam dividing the pre- and post-Spanish American War sections of her rambling barn.

She saw her sister ladling yesterday's curds into the cylinder molds Kali had bought from a retiring Provençal farmer on her last trip to the "old country." Although, truth be told, it wasn't her "old country"; it was her aunt's. But since she'd been raised by the woman with a lilting French accent, she'd adopted "ze leetle corner of heaven" as her own.

"Okay, Lacy, want to tell me what you're doing getting your hands dirty?" Kali looked at her sister's blouse and tailored jeans. "You once told me going behind the manufacturing door was not in the job description."

"Well, that was before I found out working for you included wearing four different hats. The only time I get to have any fun throwing around my executive clout is when you need me to schmooze clients." Lacy removed her apron, looping it over Kali's shoulders instead.

Kali took the ladle from her sister's inept hands and measured even spoonfuls into the molds. "Yes, but you do it so well."

Lacy wiped her hands on a terry cloth. "But I just graduated from college. I should be doing something more in line with my expensive bachelor's degree. There's bound to be a high-rise, corner office needing my skills. Don't you think?"

Kali smiled into her sister's familiar blue eyes. "It's a good thing I employed you as my business manager before Chicago or New York lured you away. Do you remember how I planned on being a corporate attorney in DC? Well, look at me now, elbow deep in goat-milk product. Progress isn't always pretty."

"I appreciate what you're doing here for the gourmet food industry," Lacy said with some disdain, "but it would appear your brain has been curdled by all this cheese."

"Because I'm not practicing law?"

Lacy folded her arms across her chest. "Don't you miss the excitement and glamour of the corporate world?"

Kali felt a tendril of hair fall from the clip holding her hair off her neck. "Some days, but mostly when the goats are acting ornery."

"But how could you throw away a six-figure salary for goats?"

"In a word? Passion." Kali looked across the room and measured her professional satisfaction not in busy suits or humming fax machines, but in creativity. "I discovered something about myself when Aunt Annalise became so ill. Life would be meaningless if on my deathbed all I had to look back on were legal documents and a bank account."

Lacy sighed. "I heard a professor say follow your heart, not your checkbook."

Kali grinned. "I bet his speech made a real impression on college seniors. If someone had told me that ten years ago, I would have said, 'Oh, get real.'"

"That's my consensus too." Lacy picked a packaging logo from the pile on the table. "So what made you do it?"

"When I took Aunt Annalise back to her family in France, I saw firsthand how hand-pressed cheese was made and how superior it was to anything I'd ever eaten in those fancy DC restaurants. And, I fell in love." Kali wiped her hands on her apron. "I loved the smell of the farm in the mornings. I loved sensing the different flavors inherent in the goat milk. I connected to the rhythm of the process. And nothing proved more satisfying than serving someone a slice of cheese and seeing their eyes close in delirious pleasure."

"Your clients never showed delirious pleasure over a favorable verdict."

"No, they usually grimaced and groaned as they wrote a check for my fees."

Lacy chuckled. "You were expensive."

"But I didn't get to see the money. It went into the corporate pot and was split among the firm. There was no conclusion for me. Of course I didn't know when I started that I'm the kind of person who needs the satisfaction of a completed cycle. And apparently I had issues with wanting to be my own boss."

"If only the goats would recognize you as their leader, that would make things even better."

"I didn't count on them being quite so stubborn. Who knew

HELLO FUTURE!

Queenie would earn her name?" Kali moved the cheese molds to a cooling rack. "But, at least when I lay my head down at night I find myself at peace because I've made something. I've fulfilled a process. And the cheese gives pleasure to others. So that makes me happy too."

Lacy helped secure the rack from rolling on the uneven floor. "I don't know that I can be happy making cheese for the rest of my life."

Kali wiped her hands on her apron before wrapping her arm around her sister's shoulders. "That's okay. Just because I'm happy with curds and whey doesn't mean you're supposed to feel the same. We're different. Even though we both grew up with Aunt Annalise singing 'Frere Jacques' doesn't mean we both like French songs. You're unique. You have your own special blend of pleasures and goals."

"But I majored in business, and I don't know what I'm supposed to do with life."

"Cut yourself some slack, Lacy. You're only twenty-two; some people don't find out their true passions until they're forty or eighty. God knits these things into our souls, but that doesn't mean they're easily discovered."

"But you found what you wanted, and you're only thirty."

Kali stepped away from Lacy, pushing her hands deep into her pockets. "It took a tragic death to help me see the difference between what made me joyful and what filled my days with occasional spurts of happiness. I spent a lot of time praying after I left France. I needed to know I wasn't walking away from a sure income because of a misguided dream. So I did both for a while. But practicing law by day and making cheese at night confirmed what

I'd already suspected about myself. I yearned to own a farm. Buying Queenie became a purposeful act and not a whim."

"So how am I going to discover my passion?" Lacy winked. "Although I haven't ruled out the glamour of corporate America as easily as you did."

"You goof," Kali chided. "Maybe corporate life is your passion. Maybe you're the kind of person that thrives on the process of putting together deals. Whatever you do, don't force the discovery of the gifts deep inside you. Let them emerge with time. Sometimes it's in the routine of life that we understand what gives us soul-satisfying pleasure."[5]

# PAUL HAMM

When Paul Hamm failed to stick his landing on the vault and crashed into the judges, his hope for winning the Olympic gold for the All Around Men's Gymnastics in Greece seemed lost. Plummeting to the number twelve spot, Paul's dream of gold sank along with his ranking. Yet in the spirit of competition, he felt he should give it his all and shoot for the bronze, though it would take both flawless floor and high bar performances to achieve that goal.

Others facing the same disappointment and frustration might have caved to the pressure, but not Paul Hamm. It had been a lifelong dream for him and his twin brother, Morgan, to make it to the Olympics and bring home a medal. Though excited to be the first set of twin gymnasts to make the Olympic team in 2000, their performances fell short of their expectations.

Four years later, accompanied by his brother again, Paul returned to the Olympics and made history by being a part of the first American team to win a medal in a non-boycotted Olympics since 1932. Though adorned with a team silver medal around his neck and proud of his team accomplishments, Paul was still hungry for gold.

After his disappointing vault, he knew his shot at the gold was lost, but the bronze was still up for grabs. Paul could have replayed his blunder over and over in his mind, yet as he mounted the high bar he focused on his routine. Around and around and around he went. Release. Catch. Release. Catch. Release. Catch. And then the dismount. The landing stuck, and the crowd went wild. It had been a near perfect routine, but was it enough for the bronze?

Thunderous cheers rang out from the crowd as the stunned Paul Hamm got the news. He had medaled and it was gold, making him the first American male ever to win the title of All-Around champion. Paul went on to win the silver medal in the individual high bar competition, overcoming yet another challenge of a rowdy crowd, making him the first American ever to win three medals in Men's Olympic Gymnastics.

Though some tried to take away his gold medal due to discrepancies in scoring, Paul Hamm knew in his heart that he was the true gold medalist for the All Around Men's Olympic Gymnastics. He had earned the spot on the American team, qualified for the finals in the All Around and, even after his ranking fell to twelfth, he still came back with a score good enough for gold. 🔥

*One thing I do: Forgetting what is behind and straining toward what is ahead, I press on toward the goal to win the prize for which God has called me heavenward in Christ Jesus.*

Philippians 3:13–14

My thoughts before a big race are usually pretty simple. I tell myself: **"Get out of the blocks, run your race, stay relaxed.** If you run your race, you'll win … Channel your energy. **Focus."**

Carl Lewis

I've always made a **total effort,** even when the odds seemed entirely against me. I **never quit trying;** I never felt that I didn't have a chance **to win.**

Arnold Palmer

**D**etermination
**E**ffort
**S**acrifice
**I**nitiative
**R**esponsibility
**E**nthusiasm

*The desire accomplished is*
*sweet to the soul.*

Proverbs 13:19 KJV

**HELLO FUTURE!**

# YOU WRITE THE SONGS

Bonnie Compton Hanson

"Mom!" Jay cried as he flew inside. "The eighth grade's having a talent contest. I want to enter! You know I love to sing. Maybe I can win some friends this way."

My smile stayed bright, but inside I sighed. Ever since we moved to this new town, Jay seemed to be a misfit. The other kids were richer, bolder, taller, more sophisticated, all one big clique. Even Jay's teachers appeared united against him.

Compared with them, Jay was the odd man out. With his growth spurt still in the future, a childish cherubic face, very shy manner, and obviously poor parents, he was way out of step with his classmates. But he did have a marvelous high voice, still unchanged.

"That's great!" I pretended. "What do you want to sing?"

"'I Write the Songs'—because I love Barry Manilow. He sings and plays the piano both. I want to write songs, too, just like he does, when I grow up. Look, could you practice with me?"

"Are you sure you don't want to use a CD or tape instead?"

His eyes shone. "No, I'd much rather have you play for me. We'll be a team."

So we practiced. And practiced. And soon he sang it so well it brought tears to my eyes.

Wait till the contest night! He'd "knock 'em dead"—and break down those puzzling walls of prejudice on his middle school campus.

The school auditorium was packed that night. As each performer sang, played, danced, or recited, large cheering sections rang out. Even though the performers were unpolished, the student team at the soundboard, under a teacher's supervision, made them sound professional. I could hardly wait for Jay's turn.

Finally they called his number. Sitting down at the piano, I joyfully played his introduction. Then he began the first note.

Suddenly a horrendous electronic squeal poured out of the amplifiers. Laughter broke out both from the soundboard operators and their in-on-the-joke teacher.

Startled, Jay faltered and looked at the judges for advice or help. "Keep right on singing, or you lose your turn," one snapped back. "No exceptions."

So he sang, even though not one of his awesome notes could be heard above the din of the amps gain. Not one parent or teacher called a halt to the shrill back-curtain guffaws which quickly spread across the audience. No one applauded my son's heroic effort. Instead, some kids yelled out, "Loser!" Then others took up the chorus. Even the judges were grinning at each other.

White as a sheet, Jay bowed and left the stage as the next contestant took the mike. Just like that, the amplifier "problems" miraculously disappeared. His humiliation was complete.

I've never felt so helpless. I could think of nothing to do or say to ease the anguish of my half-grown son.

I could hardly get him back to school the next day. The only thing that kept him going during those long hours of ridicule that day was knowing he did his best.

I wish I could say that the rest of the year was better. But it wasn't. Yet each morning he went back to school, and each evening he did his homework. He prayed and asked God for His help. He practiced. And he never gave up his dream of singing.

Then came high school. By the time he was a sophomore, ten inches taller, with a new deeper voice, and a new school, Jay blossomed. With his great voice and good looks, he soon had the lead in all the school musicals. He even became accompanist for his high school choral groups, leading them to top honors in state contests. Later he returned to his school as part of the music staff.

Today as a grown man, Jay continues to lead musical groups, to sing, to perform, to compose music. Everyone who hears him is touched and thrilled. So is he.

Maybe you, too, have been ridiculed or put down or told to give up on your dreams. Maybe your school days have sad memories that haunt you.

But, guess what? You write the songs in your life! You and God together are in charge of your dreams. Seek counselors. Ask God's help. Find friends who believe in you. Seek God's will for your life. And believe in yourself.

That's what has enabled Jay to truly "write his own songs" in life—and to sing them with joy. And you can too![6]

# AVID FOR ANIMATION

Deborah Bates Cavitt

"Mom," my son Jeff said, "I hate wearing these special glasses. I look like a freak."

Jeff was in seventh grade when he started developing eye-muscle problems. We took him to the eye doctor, and he began daily eye exercises, meeting with an eye therapist weekly, and wearing special glasses. His grades were affected, and he became restless. But there was one more reason this particular malady weighed so heavily on us. For as long as anyone could remember, Jeff had dreamed of being an animation artist—a profession that requires untold hours of close work on both hand and computer drawing.

Jeff faithfully met the daily regimen of eye exercises along with any other suggestions his doctors made. He wore the glasses—freaky looking or not—all the way through high school and junior college. But by that time, his condition was worsening. We thought his painful, bloodshot eyes might dissuade him from looking into art school—but they did not!

The doctors prescribed eyedrops throughout the day and a five-minute rest period every hour. He took the new requirements in stride and applied for art school in Florida. After all his patient endurance and hard work, Jeff graduated into a severely crippled job market. Hard times in the industry meant many computer animators were being laid off—certainly few were being hired. Interview after interview went nowhere.

Jeff was thirty-three years old before he found his dream job animating for a game company. Perseverance paid off for a young man who never let go of the dream God had placed in his heart.[7] ✷

> *Persistent people*
> **begin** *their success*
> *where others*
> **end** *in failures.*
>
> Edward Eggleston

*There are no great men in this world,*
*only great challenges which* ordinary
*men rise to meet.*

William Halsey Jr.

## *There is a potential HERO*
## *in every person.*

Oswald Chambers

When faced with a mountain, **I will not quit!** I will keep on striving until I climb over, find a pass through, tunnel underneath . . . or simply stay and turn the mountain into a gold mine, with God's help.

Robert Schuller

# JOSEPH, THE PRINCE OF EGYPT

Lavon Hightower Lewis

Joseph, the spoiled baby of the family, shot off his big mouth and told his older brothers and parents about his dream. That's when the trouble started in earnest. It was already clear to Jacob's other sons that Joseph—his child by his most beloved wife Rachel—was greatly favored by their father. A dream indicating that he would one day rule over them caused them to bristle with resentment. In those days, dreams were considered an important way for God to indicate His will. As far as Joseph's brothers were concerned, it must have felt as if God had now marked Joseph with His favor as well.

Little wonder that when the opportunity presented itself, Joseph's brothers cruelly considered killing him. Only when Reuben, the eldest of the group, begged them to spare Joseph's life did they decide to sell him to a caravan of merchants on their way to Egypt. Joseph's brothers stripped him of his multicolored robe and sent him on his way—baffled and bleeding. Then they stained the robe with blood and told their father Joseph had been killed by wild animals. There in the caravan, having been sold by his own family members into slavery, Joseph must have quickly realized that he'd lost everything—everything but his dream!

Joseph's troubles didn't stop when he got to Egypt. He was quickly sold again—this time as a house slave to a man named

HELLO FUTURE!

Potiphar. Joseph must have pulled himself together and decided to make the best of his unfortunate situation, because he soon impressed Potiphar and rose to the top position in the household. Imagine how he must have despaired when Potiphar's wife made advances and falsely accused him of attacking her.

Joseph had triumphed over his situation as a slave only to find himself enslaved in an Egyptian prison. At that point, he must have wondered if his dreams had really come from God.

There in the prison, Joseph had only the gifts God had given him. When the chief baker and the chief butler—also inmates— asked him to translate their dreams, he obliged. As he predicted, the baker was hanged. But the butler, who was returned to duty as Joseph had stated, became the key to his destiny.

Two years passed. How many moments of discouragement and despair Joseph must have endured. Finally, Pharaoh had a dream, and the butler remembered his cellmate's amazing gift. Pharaoh called for Joseph, told him about the dream he had, and said "I have heard it said of you that you can understand a dream, to interpret it." So Joseph answered Pharaoh, saying, "It is not in me; God will give Pharaoh an answer of peace" (Genesis 41:15–16 NKJV). After he interpreted the dream, he gave some recommendations on how to deal with the coming famine and suggested that a discerning and wise man be placed in charge of the land of Egypt to direct the plan for storing food.

Pharaoh said to his servants, "Can we find such a one as this, a man in whom is the Spirit of God?" Then Pharaoh said to Joseph, "Inasmuch as God has shown you all this, there is no one as discerning and wise as you" (Genesis 41:38–39 NKJV).

When Joseph's brothers went to Egypt to buy grain, they presented themselves before the second-in-command of Egypt, not knowing that he was their brother Joseph. They didn't recognize the simple boy they had sold into slavery, but he recognized them. Joseph sent his brothers back to Canaan with the grain they had requested, but he insisted on keeping one brother as security. Joseph was determined to see his brother Benjamin and his beloved father once again.

The brothers returned for Simeon and this time brought Benjamin with them. Joseph sent them back to Canaan with their grain but had his own silver cup put into his youngest brother's sack. After they left, he sent someone after them who found the cup and brought them all back. As Judah pleaded for Benjamin's life, Joseph could no longer stand it and revealed himself to them, weeping, and telling them not to be afraid. Then he sent them back to Canaan for the last time to bring their father to Egypt with the blessing of Pharaoh himself. In fact, Pharaoh told Joseph to tell his brothers, "Bring your father and your households and come to me; I will give you the best of the land of Egypt, and you will eat the fat of the land. . . . Do not be concerned about your goods, for the best of all the land of Egypt is yours" (Genesis 45:18, 20 NKJV).

God sent Joseph to Egypt so that when the famine came, there would be enough food not only for the Egyptians but Joseph's family as well so their lives would be saved. Joseph became a savior not only to the Egyptians but also to his family, the children of Israel. When Joseph was revealing himself to his brothers in Egypt, he said, "God sent me before you to preserve a posterity for you in the earth, and to save your lives by a great deliverance. So now it was not you who sent me here, but God" (Genesis 45:7–8 NKJV).

Many years later, after Jacob was dead and buried, Joseph's

brothers again approached him, asking for forgiveness, thinking that with their father gone, Joseph would bring punishment upon them for what they had done. Again Joseph wept, as he told them, "But as for you, you meant evil against me; but God meant it for good, in order to . . . save many people alive" (Genesis 50:20 NKJV).

We also see that Joseph became a prominent person in Egypt, not just because of his talents which were God-given, but more importantly, because he was a "man in whom is the Spirit of God" (Genesis 41:38 NKJV).

God gave Joseph success, prestige, honor, and wealth in Egypt, but his wealth was not just for himself alone. God had blessed him so that he would have sufficient resources to support his entire family for many years to come.

Though Joseph understood his dream to some extent, he could never have imagined how it would play out, changing his life, his brothers' lives, and even world history. Just as God used the caravan of merchants to deliver Joseph from death and take him to the place where God wanted him to be, God can use circumstances to get us to the place where God wants us to be.[8]

# Obstacles don't have to stop you. If you run into a wall, don't turn around and give up. Figure out how to climb it, go through it, or work around it.

Michael Jordan

*The heartfelt dream and the dream realized are often vastly different. The first is interpreted by our limited thinking and experience. The other is inspired by the God of magnificent miracles.*

Andrea Garney

HELLO **FUTURE!**

Dear Child,

I've heard your heart cry in the dark hours of the night. I acknowledge your anguished words: "Lord God, I have no dream. All around me people are smiling, eager to pursue one great undertaking or another, but my own heart is empty. I feel no passion. I hear no inner drummer. Please help me."

I've heard each word, and I have an answer for you.

Your heart is not empty; it only feels that way. But the heart doesn't give up its secrets easily. When your thoughts have been quieted and your panic stilled, it will begin to open to you as does a beautiful flower. Day by day, bit by bit, prayer by prayer it will spread its petals and reveal the dream I have placed there.

When your dream is finally before you, you will embrace it with fondness, as you would an old, familiar friend. You will remember what you have forgotten in the hustle and bustle of your life—a passion that has been with you from the beginning.

Give yourself time—we've got all of eternity. Do not entertain the thought that I have slighted you. I would never do that. I am your God—wise, holy, and completely just. I do not slight any of My children. I have ordained a path for each one and put within them the fire of life. Trust Me. You will not be disappointed. Rest in Me. You will not be put to shame. Your future is bright with promise.

*Your loving heavenly Father*

*Dreams are renewable.* No matter what our age or condition, there are still untapped possibilities within us and *new* beauty waiting to be born.

Dr. Dale E. Turner

# Go as far as you can see, and when you get there, *you will see farther.*

Orison Swet Marden

A dreamer dropped a random thought;

It was old, and yet was new

A simple fancy of the brain,

But strong in being true.

It shone upon a ready mind

And soon its light became

A lamp of life, a beacon ray,

An illuminating flame.

The thought was small, its issue great;

A watch-fire on the hill;

It shed its radiance far around

And cheers the valley still.

The great thing is to be found at one's post
as a child of God, living each day as
though it were our last, but planning
as though our world might last a
hundred years.

C. S. Lewis

# LIVING LIFE TO THE FULLEST

Developing a
passion for life
and realizing that
life is a gift

# YOUR FUTURE IS NOW

Your future waits before you like a beautiful song, not yet sung, but already the accompaniment is vibrating with life and pulsing with promise. How many people, both young and old, would love to be in your shoes as you stand on the cusp of your great adventure with so much to learn and experience?

It's all so exciting—and perhaps a little overwhelming as well. If you're feeling a bit apprehensive, that's all right. After all, you've been preparing for this new phase of your life for a very long time. Now that it's beginning, you'd be wrong not to give it your most sober consideration. So go ahead. Stand on the board for a while. Pause for reflection. Take your time. But when you're finally ready, don't hold back. Dive headlong into the deep end and greet your future face-first, arms outstretched in front of you, legs pulled together for a smooth entry. This life is yours, and God meant for you to live it—to the fullest.

The great clergyman Norman Vincent Peale in his book *Bible Power for Successful Living* offers these principles for getting the most out of the life you've been given:

**Live for a great purpose.** That purpose may be as unique as you are. It could be creating objects of enduring beauty, raising a godly family, making money to use in godly ways, giving hope to those in despair, or any of a limitless list of other worthy pursuits—some obscure, others in the public eye. The great anthropologist Jane Goodall chose to spend her life studying the great apes in their natural habitat—by any standard an inauspicious purpose. She spent the bulk of her life sitting in the bush, waiting and watching and taking notes. Her simple work in obscurity brought her great fame and revolutionized our understanding of how we are to deal with God's creatures.

> Pray that our God will make you
>
> fit for what he's called you to be.
>
> 2 Thessalonians 1:11 The Message

**Read the passages of joy in the Bible.** The great Russian novelist Tolstoy said that when he found God, delicious waves of life surged through his being. He enjoyed life in a totally new way. You, too, can have this joy. Read the great truths taught by Jesus in the Gospels, the words of affirmation from the Psalms and Proverbs, the encouraging optimism of the Epistles. Then simply accept God's gift of joy as you would a gift from a friend. Take joy, believe joy, live joy. Kick off this joyful way of thinking with this scripture from Isaiah:

> *You'll go out in joy,*
> *you'll be led into a whole and complete life.*
> *The mountains and hills will lead the parade,*

*bursting with song.*
*All the trees of the forest will join the procession,*
*exuberant with applause.*
*No more thistles, but giant sequoias,*
*no more thornbushes, but stately pines—*
*Monuments to me, to GOD,*
*living and lasting evidence of GOD.*

Isaiah 55:12–13 THE MESSAGE

**Practice victorious tranquility.** A quiet and calm mental attitude is easier said than done, but if you will reject worrisome thoughts and place yourself in God's hands, you can embrace tranquility. That process can become a habit, but it must first be practiced decisively—one minute, one hour, one day at a time. It's a worthy goal and one that will lead to increased creativity and productivity. As you work to overcome your anxious thoughts and behaviors and practice victorious tranquility, keep this passage in mind:

*Do not be anxious about anything, but in everything,*
*by prayer and petition, with thanksgiving, present your*
*requests to God. And the peace of God, which transcends all*
*understanding, will guard your hearts and*
*your minds in Christ Jesus.*

Philippians 4:6-7

**Avoid the things that destroy happiness.** Another key to fully living life is avoiding those things that bring unhappiness. Many things do this, but most boil down to one thing: sin. Doing what is wrong in any way simply takes the joy out of life.

Psalm 51 is a wonderful description of the effects of sin and the blessing of forgiveness. The subtitle says this is a psalm of David when the prophet Nathan faced him about his sin with Bathsheba. The story is in 2 Samuel 11.

David acknowledged his sin and begged for cleansing. He prayed, "Restore unto me the joy of thy salvation" (Psalm 51:12 KJV). He knew that when he was forgiven and restored, his happiness would return, and until then, he was not really living.

Whatever you do, if you want to be happy, avoid sin. And if you do fail, confess it and the Lord will restore to you, too, the joy of salvation.

> *Pray … that our God may count you*
> *worthy of his calling.*
> 2 Thessalonians 1:11

No sin is small. No grain of sand is small in the mechanism of a watch.

Jeremy Taylor

**Bring happiness to others; it will rub off on you.**
Real living is giving. Remember that, and you will never lose your
sense of excitement about life. The great writer James Barrie said,
"Those who bring sunshine to the lives of others cannot keep it
from themselves."

In the epistle of James, we see how to find joy even in our
troubles. James points the way to the abiding joy of the Lord. It is
what real religion is all about:

> *Pure religion and undefiled before God and*
> *the Father is this, To visit the fatherless and widows in*
> *their affliction, and to keep himself unspotted*
> *from the world.*
>
> James 1:27 KJV

Genuine religion, then—and a profound way to happiness and
fulfillment—is helping those in need and keeping so deeply in tune
with God's purposes that the false values of the world are unable to
stain or defile us.

**Try the seven-day mental diet, refusing to say anything negative for one week.** Emmet Fox, a student of Scripture, produced a small pamphlet in which he introduced a seven-day mental diet. The idea is this: Resolve that for exactly one week you will watch every word as a cat watches a mouse. For those seven days, refuse to say one mean or dishonest or depressing thing, no matter what thoughts enter your head.

This may not be an easy proposition. It's common to try several times before you succeed. But you'll get there if you ask for God's help and refuse to give up—and the benefits are great. Such a seven-day program of eliminating the negative and programming mind and heart for the positive will bring you a rise to the heights of happiness and the ability to live every moment of your life with passion and purpose.

*Finally, my friends,* keep your minds on whatever is *true, pure, right, holy, friendly, and proper.* Don't ever stop thinking about what is truly worthwhile and worthy of praise.

Philippians 4:8 CEV

**HELLO FUTURE!**

*Be transformed by the renewing of your mind. Then you will be able to test and approve what God's will is—his good, pleasing and perfect will.*

Romans 12:2

**Walk with the Lord of joy and live in His Spirit.**
For the fullest possible life, give yourself completely to the Master
of joy. Trust your whole being to Him. Read His words in the Bible,
follow His ways, talk to Him in prayer. As you do, He will irradiate
your personality with "joy unspeakable and full of glory" (1 Peter
1:8 KJV), while energizing your life to an extent you may never have
dreamed possible.

*You have made known to me the paths of life;*
*you will fill me with joy in your presence.*

Acts 2:28

*Life is filled with meaning as soon as Jesus*
*Christ enters into it.*

Bishop Stephen Charles Neill

I will not just live my life.
I will not just spend my life.
I will invest my life.

Helen Adams Keller

**Making good choices is the key to living a rich, full life.** That sounds simple enough, and it would be if it weren't for the sheer number of choices to be made. You will be asked to decide how to spend your time, your energy, and what you hope to accomplish in your life. Those choices—the big ones and the little ones—can be intimidating—unless they are addressed in the context of godly character. Consider these tips for making good life choices:

1. Pursue God's goals for your life, not your own goals.

2. Spurn pride; walk in humility.

3. Service and charity to others is required of us all.

4. Right and wrong are absolute; integrity matters.

5. A useful life is more important than a comfortable life.

6. God first; then family. God will never ask you to neglect your family.

7. If you believe everything you read, you'd do better not to read.

8. It is allowable to learn—even from an enemy.

9. Love peace, but love truth even more.

10. Patience is power.

11. Worry gives a small thing a big shadow.

12. If you want your dreams to come true, don't sleep.

13. Begin too much, and you will accomplish little.

14. What soap is to the body, tears of repentance are to the soul.

15. Love begets love.

16. Money will be your master—or your slave.

17. If there is light in the soul, there will be beauty in the person.

18. Evil is overcome by good.

19. Appearances can be deceiving.

20. You never know the worth of water until the well is dry.

The world is a large and wonderful place, and it is your time to step into it boldly. Don't get stuck on idle—move out, make choices, based on the best possible information you have. Listen to the voice of the Holy Spirit, embrace the principles for right living contained in God's Word, seek godly counsel, and learn the principles of righteousness. When you choose in favor of godliness, you will never have a misstep.

"Cheshire Puss," she began, rather timidly, as she did not at all know whether it would like the name: however, it only grinned a little wider. "Come, it's pleased so far," thought Alice, and she went on. "Would you tell me, please, which way I ought to go from here?"

"That depends a good deal on where you want to get to," said the Cat.

"I don't much care where—" said Alice.

"Then it doesn't matter which way you go," said the Cat.

"—so long as I get *somewhere*," Alice added as an explanation.

"Oh, you're sure to do that," said the Cat, "if you only walk long enough."

Lewis Carroll
*Alice's Adventure in Wonderland*

**HELLO FUTURE!**

# Fifteen Simple Admonitions for Passionate Living

1. Count your blessings, not your troubles.

2. Learn to live one day at a time.

3. Learn to say, "I love you," "Thank you," and "I appreciate you."

4. Learn to be a giver and not a getter.

5. Seek the good in everyone and everything.

6. Pray every day.

7. Do at least one good deed every day.

8. Put God first.

9. Let nothing bother you.

10. Practice the "Do it now" habit.

11. Fill your life with good.

12. Learn to laugh and learn to cry.

13. Learn to practice the happiness habit.

14. Learn to fear nothing and no one.

15. Learn to let go and let God.

*[Jesus said,] "The thief's purpose is to steal and kill and destroy. My purpose is to give life in all its fullness."*

John 10:10 NLT

---

If death got the upper hand through one man's wrongdoing, can you imagine the breathtaking recovery life makes, sovereign life, in those who grasp with both hands this wildly extravagant life-gift, this grand setting-everything-right, that the one man Jesus Christ provides?

Romans 5:17 THE MESSAGE

---

**HELLO FUTURE!**

*May grace and peace be yours in abundance in the knowledge of God and of Jesus our Lord.*

2 Peter 1:2 NRSV

Beloved One:

Not only have I given you life—but I've given it to you with no strings attached. You decide how it will be lived. You must make the decision to extract every moment of goodness and beauty and insight or—by default—you will simply use up your days going through the motions.

Of course, My will for you is to live an abundant life. But I don't want you to be confused. An abundant life does not just mean plenty of money and possessions. It means your heart is full of good things, your mind is accessing wisdom, knowledge, and creativity, and your soul is satisfied in terms of love, joy, and peace.

You must know by now that the world is not set up to give you an abundant life. Instead, it is likely to take what you have and leave you with nothing but unhappiness, frustration, and emptiness. Abundant living comes only through your relationship with Me—your Creator. No one knows you better—your unique perspective on life, your gifts and talents, your deepest needs. I can guide you through the ambiguities and confusion as together we create something wonderful—but I won't intrude on your life. You must invite Me in, make a place for Me. Until then, I'll be waiting.

*Your heavenly Father*

# To live means to have a mission to fulfill—and in the measure in which we avoid setting our life to something, we make it empty.

José Ortega y Gasset

Unless you give yourself to some great cause, you haven't even begun to live.

William P. Merrill

Be a life long or short, *its completeness depends on what it was lived for.*

David Starr Jordan

HELLO FUTURE!

**Do not come to the end of your life only to find that you have not lived.** *For many come to the point of leaving the space of the earth, and when they gaze back, they see the joy and the beauty that could **not** be theirs because of the fears they lived.*

*Clearwater*

# SOUL SINGER AND MINISTER AL GREEN

One of the most enduring soul singers of all time, Al Green was and is a legend to his fans, noted for hits such as "Let's Stay Together," "I'm Still in Love with You," and "Tired of Being Alone." Even though they were recorded in the '70s, they are still loved, played, and enjoyed by millions. You might think that having been given such a remarkable gift, Al Green's life would be all about music. For a while it was. But when Al came face-to-face with God's purpose for his life, he became a servant of God first and a singer second. Only God's plan allowed him to live life to the fullest.

Al Green was raised in a no-nonsense Christian home, where he grew up singing for the Lord. Secular music was considered inappropriate and worldly. If his parents had had their way, Al would never have spread his wings beyond the bounds of gospel music. But by late in his high school years, he was able to join up with some friends and start a band called Al Green and the Soul Mates. It was the beginning of a meteoric rise to fame beyond his wildest dreams.

Unprecedented success came quickly and stayed. Al found no real conflict with the music, just the trappings—too much money, women, drugs. Nothing was withheld from him. He could have anything he wanted. But something was missing. Al Green knew he was not living life to the fullest.

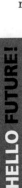

Then one night at a Disneyland hotel, Green says he woke a changed man. He says that while he slept, God had snatched him out of his dark world and placed him into relationship with Him. "I woke up born again," he told a television audience. Al's transformation was a lasting one. Leaving this music career, he became a minister of God's love and truth. He's now known as Pastor Green, and he says that he has never been more fully alive.

In recent times, Green remains the pastor of the church God led him to begin, but he feels he is now ready to reach out and produce the beautiful secular melodies his fans have so long loved. But this time, he will not be confused or corrupted by the trappings of fame. He knows that God is the source and sustainer of his life.

Life is more than money, fame, and possessions. It is a gift from God. To live your life to the fullest, you will need to submit your gifts and talents to Him. Only then will you know what it is to live with meaning and purpose. 🔥

# Wisdom is sweet to your soul; if you find it, there is a future hope for you, and your hope will not be cut off.

**Proverbs 24:14**

Dear Friend:

Taking hold of your future is like standing poised at the beginning of a race—foot securely anchored in the block, arms in their forward position, knees slightly bent, head held up and forward, eyes on the finish line. Every muscle, every joint, every thought waits to hear the starting shot that will launch the runner out into the midst of the competition and on to the finish line.

For so long you've been preparing for your future, your mind becoming more and more preoccupied with the technicalities of the race itself. You've been busy getting a firm grip on your race strategy, collecting the proper equipment, scoping out the competition, getting yourself in shape mentally and physically—all so you can blast out of that starting block ahead of the pack. You may have concluded that there's only one way to run the race of life—fast!

It might be more appropriate to determine to run your race well, rather than just fast. You may need to consider that crossing the finish line is only one part of the race, the final part. If just getting to the end first is your only consideration, imagine what you will miss.

Your future stands before you—waiting. It's filled with relationships—God, family, and friends—as well as personal growth, moments of joy and happiness, smaller victories along the way, and an abundance of love and peace and blessing. Run your race with vigor, but don't let it keep you from living your life to the fullest.

Best regards,

*Andrea*

Do you not know that in a race all the runners run, but only one gets the prize? Run in such a way as to get the prize. Everyone who competes in the games goes into strict training. They do it to get a crown that will not last; but we do it to get a crown that will last forever.

1 Corinthians 9:24–25

*The most important thing in the Olympic Games is not winning but taking part. . . . The essential thing in life is not conquering but fighting well.*

Pierre de Coubertin

Speech to Officials of the Olympic Games, 24 July 1908

Live while you live, the epicure would say,

And seize the pleasure of the present day;

Live while you live, the sacred preacher cries,

And give to God each moment as it flies.

Lord, in my views, let both united be:

**I live in pleasure when
I live to thee.**

Philip Doddridge

Epigraph on His Family Arms

# EDUCATION

Edgar A. Guest

*There is an education of the mind*

*Which all require and parents early start,*

*But there is training of a nobler kind*

*And that's the education of the heart.*

*Lessons that are most difficult to give*

*Are faith and courage and the way to live.*

# Twenty-four Things to Remember—and One Never to Forget

1. Remember that ... your presence is a present to the world.

2. Remember that ... you're unique and one of a kind.

3. Remember that ... your life can be whatever you want it to be.

4. Remember that ... it's best to take each day as it comes.

5. Remember that ... you should count your blessings, not your troubles.

6. Remember that ... God will help you through whatever comes.

7. Remember that ... God has the answer to any question you may have.

8. Remember that ... you should never put limits on yourself.

9. Remember that ... you must have courage and be strong.

10. Remember that ... you have many dreams waiting to be realized.

11. Remember that ... only you can fulfill your dreams.

12. Remember that ... decisions are too important to leave to chance.

13. Remember that ... it's up to you to reach for your peak, your goal, and your prize.

14. Remember that ... nothing wastes more time than worrying.

15. Remember that ... the longer you carry a problem, the heavier it gets.

16. Remember that ... you should never take things too seriously.

17. Remember that ... you should live in a way that leaves you with no regrets.

18. Remember that ... a little love goes a long way.

19. Remember that ... you should never ever give up!

20. Remember that ... friendship is one of life's wisest investments.

21. Remember that ... life's treasures are people.

22. Remember that ... it's never too late.

23. Remember that ... ordinary things can be done in extraordinary ways.

24. Remember that ... health, hope, and happiness are worth striving for.

**And never forget ... how very special you are!**

**The person who succeeds** is not the one who holds back, fearing failure, nor the one who never fails ... but rather the one who moves on in spite of failure.

Charles R. Swindoll

The most effective way to ensure the value of the future is to confront the present courageously and constructively.

Rollo May

HELLO FUTURE!

*Don't waste your time living someone else's life. Don't be trapped by dogma—which is living with the results of other people's thinking. Don't let the noise of others' opinions drown out your own inner voice. And most important,* have the courage to follow your heart and intuition. *They somehow already know what you truly want to become.*

*Everything else is secondary.*

Steve Jobs
CEO of Apple Computer and Pixar Animation Studios
Commencement Speech 2005

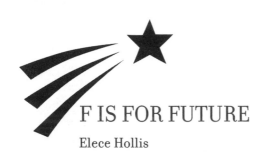

# F IS FOR FUTURE

Elece Hollis

I stared in disbelief at the red ink dripped like blood all over the pages—a large red F at the top screamed at me. She had done it again! She got me! How unfair!

I loved literature in high school. My literature book introduced me to new and exciting authors to read and love. It introduced me to the desire to become a writer. The prospect of writing made my heart race. For a shy girl from a family of eleven, this was an opportunity to speak up at last—if not aloud, at least on paper. So I took composition, and as a senior I got the formidable Mrs. Cox.

Mrs. Cox wore Coke-bottle-bottom glasses. She was as austere and short as her name. I had never seen her smile, but I imagined that she smiled slightly when she graded her students' papers and found errors she could mark with her sharpened and waiting red pencils. This was her great joy in life!

She frowned properly while returning our devastated compositions to watch the dismay wash over our faces. Maybe then she was actually laughing a wicked witch's "naa-ha-ha-ha-ha" inside, but was too prim and proper to let it out.

I determined to beat her at the game. I knew I could write a nice outline and a star essay with no errors for her to delight in. I wrote, rewrote, edited, and revised the piece. No fear! I knew it was good and turned it in in full confidence that I would finally get the A I deserved.

We got the essays back the next Monday morning. The corner of Mrs. Cox's mouth crimped into an almost smile as she called my name.

She was impressed all right. I had finally outwitted her and given her an essay she would have to admire—one she could find no fault in.

I went up to retrieve mine, walked smugly to my seat without looking at it, and then gasped as I turned the paper over. My face colored to the red of the ink encircling several words in each sentence, the 59 at the top beside the boisterous F.

My best paper yet, and my worst grade.

I was confused and then furious. These words were not misspelled, but each was marked with a neat sp. I had checked any word I had been unsure of. I had won spelling bees in grade school, for heaven's sake. There were forty-one words circled, and many of them were simple words: *did, time, first, it, bright, sigh,* and *trim.*

I, the shy one, scheduled a conference, and, shaking with frustration, I sat across from my teacher. "Why are all these words marked for spelling? I don't understand."

She took the paper from me and glanced over it before she handed it back. "You have placed your dots too far from the tops of your i's; therefore the words are misspelled. There are forty-one of them. That makes a score of fifty-nine, and in my class, fifty-nine is an F."

There was no comment on the essay, on the content, or even on the sentence structure. *Bizarre! Maybe she just hates me for some reason and hopes I will fail,* I thought and left the room shaking my head. I had to go on writing, even though I felt I was unfairly treated, so I accepted the grade and practiced to overcome my horrendous penmanship flaw. Through the remainder of high school and college, while other students minded their p's and q's, I minded my i's and j's. I dotted each precisely.

Now that I am a teacher myself, I remember the lesson Mrs. Cox taught me. Dots count, I learned. "Writing" would be "wrtng" without them. I can now appreciate the importance of detail in penmanship, spelling, and punctuation as well as content.

Thank you, Mrs. Cox, for insisting on a level of excellence I would not have gained without you. Thank you for an F that helped to shape my future!

The goal of life is imminent in each moment—each thought, word, act—and does not have to be sought apart from these. It consists in no specific achievement, but the state of mind in which everything is done, the quality infused into existence. The function of each person is not to attain an object, but to fulfill a purpose; not to accomplish but to be accomplished.[9]

# The work of life alone teaches us to value the good of life.

Author Unknown

Be not afraid of life. Believe that life is worth living, and your belief will help create the fact.

Bruyère

●

*If we are ever to enjoy life, now is the time— not tomorrow, nor next year, nor in some future life after we have died. The best preparation for a better life next year is a full, complete, harmonious, joyous life this year. Our beliefs in a rich future life are of little importance unless we coin them into a rich present life. Today should always be our most wonderful day.*

Thomas Dreier

**Life is more** than eating and drinking, more than buying and selling, more than getting and spending, more than the cultivation of the mind and a healthy body. **It is the widening of our horizon, the broadening of our vision, the reaching out to eternal realities, the discipline of self.**

E. Clowes Chorley

Be glad of life
because it gives you the chance to love
and to work and to play and
to look at the stars.

Henry Van Dyke

*Live your life each day
as you would climb a mountain.
An occasional glance toward the summit
keeps the goal in mind, but many beautiful
scenes are to be observed from each new
vantage point.* Climb slowly, steadily,
enjoying each passing moment;
**and the view from the
summit will serve as a fitting
climax for the journey.**

Harold Melchert

Someone has well said,

"Success is a journey, not a destination."

Happiness is to be found along the way,

not at the end of the road. **Today,**

**this hour, this minute is the day, is**

**the hour, the minute for each of us to**

**sense the fact that life is good,** with

all of its trials and troubles, and

perhaps more interesting

because of them.

Robert Updegraff

1. Do more than exist, *live.*
2. Do more than touch, *feel.*
3. Do more than look, *observe.*
4. Do more than read, *absorb.*
5. Do more than hear, *listen.*
6. Do more than listen, *understand.*
7. Do more than think, *ponder.*
8. Do more than talk, *say something.*

John H. Rhoades

## Your future begins today!

**Author Unknown**

*I will give them a heart to know me,*
*that I am the* LORD.

Jeremiah 24:7

# PURSUING YOUR GOD

Cultivating a relationship
with the One who
loves you most

# YOUR FUTURE IS NOW

You've probably been told that there are no guarantees in life. The future is a blank template—your story being written as you pass from moment to moment. That concept is both wholly right and wholly wrong. You certainly are responsible for the direction your life takes; choices build upon choices, patterns of choices upon patterns of choices leading the way before you. Your past and your present really do shape your future.

That would be that—flat out, pure and simple—except for one thing. Our lives, though steered by our choices, are not initiated by our choice. We have a Creator! And He is wise enough and powerful enough to alter the course of our lives at any point. He sees our lives, though yet unlived, from beginning to end. Best of all, He has taken the time to establish a plan for every person, including you—a plan consistent with the gifts and talents He has placed in you. That God-alternative is what we know as God's will.

God has a plan for your life, but He has given you the right to choose His will or continue on in your own way. If you go your own way, you'll have no guarantees. If you go God's way, you'll have many guarantees:

1. You will never be alone. (See Hebrews 13:5.)

2. Past mistakes will be forgiven. (See 1 John 1:9.)

3. You will be guided by the wisdom and counsel of God's Holy Spirit. (See Proverbs 4:11.)

4. You will never be without love. (See Lamentations 3:32–33.)

5. You will have eternal life. (See 1 John 2:17.)

6. Your life will count for something. (See Psalm 33:11.)

7. You will have peace. (See Romans 8:6.)

8. You will have joy. (See Psalm 16:11.)

9. You will have strength. (See Philippians 4:13.)

10. You will be blessed. (See John 1:16.)

And this is the short list. Your life surrendered to the will of God may not—probably won't—be an easy life, but it is one that will give you a future and a hope!

*The past, the present and the future are really one—they are today.*

Harriet Beecher Stowe

My Dear One:

As you launch out into the world, so many choices await you: where to live, what job to take, possibly who to marry. It's an exciting time, filled with possibility. Yet, above all, the most important choice you'll make is this: Who will you serve?

Everyone serves something or someone in his or her life. For many, this is money. It's a choice the world encourages, even applauds. On its altar, many have sacrificed every-thing—family, friends, even their personal integrity. Yet money is a grim taskmaster—never satisfied, always promis-ing more. And those who pursue it above all else find only disillusionment and emptiness.

Instead, I hope you'll choose a higher purpose: to know Me more intimately—to make our relationship a priority—even when the world tries to seduce you away.

My love for you never fails; My kindnesses—and forgive-ness—are new every morning when you wake. Come to Me every day, and let Me comfort and encourage you. Pursue Me—I promise I'll never disappoint you or leave you empty.

*Your heavenly Father*

*I have swept away*

*your offenses like a cloud,*

*your sins like the morning mist.*

*Return to me,*

*for I have redeemed you.*

Isaiah 44:22

Walk quietly—

and know that He is God. Let your life be governed by His guiding hand even though it varies from the way you planned. Bow your head in sweet submission and walk quietly.

Author Unknown

Commit to the LORD whatever you do, and your plans will succeed.

Proverbs 16:3

Dear Friend:

You have something that God wants. Does that surprise you? Listen to what God says in His Word: "My child, give me your heart" (Proverbs 23:26 NRSV).

Now, there are two things I wish to talk about in connection with these words.

The first is: What does it mean to give your heart to God?

The second is: Why should you give your heart to Him?

Did you notice that God does not ask you to give Him your head, nor your hands, nor your feet. Do you find this strange? Yet there is a reason for it. What do you do with your head? You think with it. What do you do with your hands? You work with them. What do you do with your feet? You walk with them. But you don't do any of those things with your heart; that is not what your heart is for.

Imagine a little boy who has just returned to his home. He finds his father there. He runs to him and throws his arms around his neck, and says, "Oh, my dear father, I do love you with all my—"
What?—Why, heart, to be sure!

Then what is it that you do with your heart? Why, you love with it. Yes, your heart was made for this. The heart is the seat or place of the affections.

But, my friend, it is not the literal heart that God wants. He speaks of the heart here as a figure of speech, as the place where your affections lie; and what He wants you to give Him is not the fleshly heart out of your body, but the affections that are seated in that figurative heart. When He says, "My child, give Me your heart," He means, "My child, give Me your love; give Me your devotion; set your hopes and dreams on Me; love Me above all else."

This is what God means when He says, "My child, give Me your heart."

This is the answer to the first question that we proposed—what does it mean to give your heart to God?

The second question is: Why should you give your heart to God?

There are two reasons for this.

In the first place, you should give your heart to God because He has the right to it. He made your heart for Himself, and it belongs to Him. God designed it to be a place where He can dwell. Nothing else can fill that place inside you. Unless God fills it, you will never be happy—in this world or in the world to come. And if God made your heart on purpose that you might love Him with it, surely this is the best reason in the world for you to give it to Him.

Suppose a little girl should spend a holiday in dressing her doll, or a little boy in making a kite or a boat, and just when they were finished—the doll all dressed, looking very sweet, and the kite ready to fly or the boat to sail—someone should come along and take it away by force: how wrong would that be?

Suppose a gentleman should build himself a beautiful house and fit it up for his own use, and, just as he was getting ready to move into it and live there, one of his neighbors should get in, and not be willing to let him enter and live in the house that he made for himself. How unjust would that be? Such interlopers would be called robbers.

Just so it is, my dear friend, with your heart. God made it for Himself. He desires to come in and dwell in it. He wishes to possess your love and affections. He wants you to love Him above all else.

He says in one place in the Bible, "Here I am! I stand at the door [of your heart] and knock. If anyone hears my voice and opens the door, I will come in and eat with him, and he with me" (Revelation 3:20). But until you are ready to give your heart to God—to set your affections on Him—you are unwilling to let Him come in and dwell in the place He made for Himself. Surely this is robbing God—robbing Him of that which He desires to possess above all things—the one thing He wants from you![10]

As one who has gone on before,

*Rev. Richard Newton*

*My child, give me your heart.*

Proverbs 23:26 NRSV

God wants to be loved for Himself and honored for Himself, but that is only part of what He wants. The other part is that He wants us to know that when we have Him, we have everything—we have all the rest.

A. W. Tozer

The idea that you have to "find God" is a misconception. God, after all, is not lost. He is where He has always been—right by your side. You can't see Him—don't recognize His hand moving in your life because the eyes of your soul have been blinded by sin and unbelief. God wants to remove the blinders and open your spiritual eyes. He wants you to know Him. He has already done the work and paid the price. Now He waits for your response. You must make a decision, exercise your free will, and say to Him, "Father God, I want to know You. Forgive my sin and wash me clean inside. Remove the blinders from the eyes of my soul, and by Your resurrection power give me new life."

*We do not walk to God with the feet of our body, nor would wings, if we had them, carry us to Him, but we go to Him by the affections of our soul.*

Saint Augustine

These five steps can help you establish a firm connection with God who loves you and wants you to
know Him:

1.  Come to Him just as you are. Don't wait until
you feel "good enough" because you never will.
Even if you were capable of cleaning up your
life, your determination would be futile. God's
glory requires more than a good job; it requires
perfection, and human beings simply don't have
the means to achieve perfection. Instead, they
must be "made perfect" by God Himself. (See
Titus 3:5.)

2.  Admit your need. No matter how great or
small your sin, you are a sinner—we all are.
You need God's help—we all do. (See Romans
3:21–27.)

3.  Be willing to turn away from your sin.
Repentance is a big word for a simple action—
turning around and going the other way. Your
thoughts, your actions, your attitudes have
turned your attention away from God and
His purpose for your life. They have kept you
focused on self, rather than on God. Since you
cannot save yourself, your only hope is to focus
on God and the sacrifice of His Son, Jesus—your
Savior. (See Acts 3:19.)

4. Believe with all your heart that Jesus is the Son of God, that He died on the cross for your sins and was raised back to life. You must clearly understand that He is the only way to God. (See 1 Timothy 2:5–6; Acts 4:12.)

5. Act on the understanding that Jesus died for everyone—but very specifically, He died for you. Receive His sacrifice on your behalf and invite Him into your heart. (See Revelation 3:20.)

> Ever since the days of Adam, man has been hiding from God and saying, "God is hard to find."
>
> Fulton J. Sheen

*We think we must climb to a certain height of goodness before we can reach God. But if we are in a hole, the Way begins in the hole. The moment we set our face in the same direction as His, we are walking with God.*

Helen Wodehouse

> If we get our information from the biblical material **there is no doubt that the Christian life is a** dancing, leaping, daring life.
>
> Eugene Peterson

Now that you've acted upon your desire to know God and made certain of your standing in His eyes—now that the blindness of sin has been washed from your eyes and you can see clearly—it's time to explore the wonder, the greatness, the miracle of your relationship with almighty God.

The consummate scholar-pastor Eugene Peterson is best known not for his years as a pastor, but for his translation of the entire Bible into everyday American English. This translation, called *The Message*, draws on a strong working understanding of the biblical languages. Whether you are a new Christian or have been following Christ for many years, this passage from the book of Ephesians, chapter 2, verses 1–13, gives a wonderful bird's-eye view of your status as God's child:

**HELLO FUTURE!**

*It wasn't so long ago that you were mired in that old stagnant life of sin. You let the world, which doesn't know the first thing about living, tell you how to live. You filled your lungs with polluted unbelief, and then exhaled disobedience. We all did it, all of us doing what we felt like doing, when we felt like doing it, all of us in the same boat. It's a wonder God didn't lose his temper and do away with the whole lot of us. Instead, immense in mercy and with an incredible love, he embraced us. He took our sin-dead lives and made us alive in Christ. He did all this on his own, with no help from us! Then he picked us up and set us down in highest heaven in company with Jesus, our Messiah.*

*Now God has us where he wants us, with all the time in this world and the next to shower grace and kindness upon us in Christ Jesus. Saving is all his idea, and all his work. All we do is trust him enough to let him do it. It's God's gift from start to finish! We don't play the major role. If we did, we'd probably go around bragging that we'd done the whole thing! No, we neither make nor save ourselves. God does both the making and saving. He creates each of us by Christ Jesus to join him in the work he does, the good work he has gotten ready for us to do, work we had better be doing.*

*But don't take any of this for granted. It was only yesterday that you outsiders to God's ways had no idea of any of this, didn't know the first thing about the way God works, hadn't the faintest idea of Christ. You knew nothing of that rich history of God's covenants and promises in Israel, hadn't a clue about what God was doing in the world at large. Now, because of Christ—dying that death, shedding that blood—you who were once out of it altogether are in on everything.*

So then, just as you received Christ Jesus as Lord, **continue** to live in him, **rooted and built up** in him, **strengthened** in the faith as you were taught, and **overflowing** with thankfulness.

Colossians 2:6–7

HELLO **FUTURE!**

We do not segment our lives, giving some time to God, some to our business or schooling, while keeping parts to ourselves. *The idea is to live all of our lives in the presence of God, under the authority of God, and for the honor and glory of God.* **That is what the Christian life is all about.**

R. C. Sproul

## SIX WAYS TO GROW IN YOUR RELATIONSHIP WITH GOD

1. **Maintain a grateful heart.** It's easy to begin to take your faith and the extraordinary nature of your relationship with God for granted. Just as people who are successful in marriage strive to keep the memory and fire of their first love alive in their hearts, you must do the same. Each morning and each night, thank God for what He has done for you through the sacrifice of His Son, Jesus. Thank Him for making you His child. Thank Him for loving you. (See Hebrews 12:28.)

2. **Share God's love.** Telling others what God has done for you reinforces the power of it in your own life. It may also be the one voice that leads another person to ask God to open his or her spiritual eyes. (See Colossians 1:28.)

3. **Seek friends in the faith.** It's important to have friends who will encourage you as you grow spiritually and pray for you when you wander off the path. (See Ephesians 4:29.)

4. **Practice doing the right thing.** As God's child, you are bound by honor. No longer should you allow yourself to behave without regard for your position. It no longer matters if you can get away with it, it doesn't hurt anyone, or others are doing it. You do what's right because it pleases your heavenly Father and because you represent Him to the world. (See Psalm 37:30–31.)

5. **Pray, pray, pray.** Now that you have established a conversation with God, don't ever let it end. It should be a running conversation, facilitated by the Holy Spirit who now lives inside your heart. There will be times of formal prayer, of course. But those should be viewed as structured talks within the context of an ongoing interaction between you and God. (See 1 Thessalonians 5:17; Ephesians 6:18.)

6. **Read the Bible.** God knew it would be a challenge for you to live a spiritual life in a material world. That's why He provided a manual for you to live by. The wisdom you will find inside the Bible is timeless, always relevant. The stories you read are about real people, who lived, loved, and made mistakes. It is a history of God's interaction with you from the time of creation to times yet to come. Keep it near you, read it often, mark it up. (See 2 Timothy 3:16–17.)

## FIVE CONDITIONS FOR EFFECTIVE PRAYER

1. **You must be completely dependent on the Lord Jesus for your standing before your heavenly Father.** You deserve nothing from Him on your own merits. Thinking that you have done something good, so He owes you, is a bogus concept. God owes you nothing—but He will give you everything you ask if you ask properly.

2. **You must not be giving place to sin in your life.** It's true that God is gracious and merciful, but He will not reward willful sin. God will not help you hurt yourself. When you willfully sin, that's exactly what you are doing. You're acting in opposition to your own self-interests. God loves you too much to approve that.

3. **You must have faith in God's promises.** If you don't believe that God can help, that He will answer, that He cares, you will never be able to receive what you ask for. That's what faith is all about.

4. **You must ask in accordance with His will.** God wants so much for you. He will not answer a prayer that will lead you other than to the center of His will.

5. **You must wait for the answer.** God is not on your schedule. Still, He can be trusted. He knows exactly when the answer should come. Trust Him.

Prayer really is just conversation with God. It often takes several conversations with Him before you can secure the answer. God is patient, however. He likes to work with you, bringing you to the place where you can pray wisely and effectively.

## EIGHT TIPS FOR EFFECTIVE BIBLE STUDY

The Bible is such a big part of cultivating your relationship with God. It is a well of living water so deep that a bucket on the longest rope will never touch the bottom. If you studied for the entirety of your lifetime, you would still find something new within its pages each time you open it. That's because it is no ordinary book. It's a miraculous book, filled with the living, breathing words of God. It is the best possible way to pursue your future, discover God's will, and live a life of purpose. Try these tips for effective Bible study.

1. **Choose a version you are comfortable with.** Not so long ago there was only one English version of the Bible—the King James. Now, however, there are literally dozens of versions, some translations and some paraphrases. Consider some of these popular versions:

   - **Revised Standard Version and New Revised Standard Version.** The RSV was published in 1952, and it retains much of the beautiful language of the King James Version, but its vocabulary has become dated. The NRSV corrects this deficiency and so drops the "man" gender reference.

   - **New International Version and the Today's New International Version.** The NIV is practically considered the standard these days. It is thought to be a very balanced translation, adhering closely to the Hebrew and Greek original text. The TNIV, its latest update, is a good option as well.

- **New King James Version.** The NKJV stays closer to the language of the King James Version than many other translations, retaining much of the beautiful style of the KJV.

- **The Living Bible.** Referred to as the TLB, this version is not really a translation but a paraphrase. It was an attempt by one person to put the Bible into a form his children could understand. While lacking some scholarly acumen, it is an excellent Bible for beginners.

- **The Message.** THE MESSAGE is one of the brightest paraphrased versions on the market. Its lively language really connects with youthful readers. You won't have trouble staying with this one.

2. **Take some time to get to know your Bible.** Check out the materials in the front and back of your new Bible, as well as the margin notes. Is there a concordance, dictionary, atlas, or maps? There should be a full explanation of these helps in the introduction. If you aren't already able to recite the books of the Bible, begin with the New Testament and keep working until you have committed them to memory. This will be a project in itself, but you will be glad you did it. Practice by looking up verses at random (what are called "Bible drills") using the contents page of your Bible for reference. Reading through the Bible will also help you learn each book's place in relation to the whole.

3. **Choose a systematic plan for reading through the Bible.** You will have no trouble finding a Bible reading plan online, but you can easily develop your own. Simply take one chapter per day and use this format:

|           | Week One:                        | Week Two:                        |
|-----------|----------------------------------|----------------------------------|
| Day One   | Genesis 1                        | Genesis 2                        |
| Day Two   | Psalm 1                          | Psalm 2                          |
| Day Three | Isaiah 1                         | Isaiah 2                         |
| Day Four  | Matthew 1                        | Matthew 2                        |
| Day Five  | Romans 1                         | Romans 2                         |
| Day Six   | Review Old Testament readings    | Review Old Testament readings    |
| Day Seven | Review New Testament readings    | Review New Testament readings    |

When you complete a book, move on to the next until you reach the first book of the next section. Then return to the first book of that section and begin again. Some sections will be completed long before others, and you will read the New Testament more than twice before you have read the Old Testament once.

4. **Choose a good time to read each day.** It isn't necessary to choose a specific time. In fact this could begin to feel restrictive, and Bible reading should feel refreshing. Instead, choose a "time of day" to read—morning, afternoon, evening, right before going to sleep, as soon as you get up in the morning. People are different. You may be bright and perky in the morning and a sleepyhead at night. Or it could be just the other way around. Schedule your Bible reading for a time when you are usually alert and at your best. You will soon begin to look forward to your time in God's Word.

5. **Ask God to refresh, instruct, correct, and inspire you as you read.** The Holy Spirit has prom-

ised to do just that, and taking a moment for prayer will help settle your mind and make you more receptive.

6. **Read your daily chapter twice—once for your head and once for your heart**. In the first reading your mind will be taking note of the sequence of events, characters, and major themes. Your second reading will allow you to see the spiritual principles and concepts resident in the reading.

7. **Keep a pen and notebook or journal with your Bible.** God has promised to give you insights and understanding as you read His Word. When that happens, write it down and date it. Writing it out will reinforce the principle in your mind and heart. This is particularly important as you review at the end of each week. Also record questions so that you can seek understanding from your parents, pastor, or Sunday school teacher, or use a Bible aid to help you find the answer.

8. **Share what you've learned with others.** The blessings you receive from reading God's Word are worthy of being shared with others. Not only will it increase their understanding, but it will reinforce God's truth in your own spirit.

Initiating your relationship with God and learning how to cultivate it in your life is the first step to achieving God's will and purpose for your life. It's the first step to success, prosperity, and happiness. It's the first step to a future of joy, peace, and fellowship with the best Friend you will ever have.

Dear Friend:

I'll bet if I asked you who your closest friends are, you could rattle off a list of names quickly. These are more than just acquaintances; these are the people who've seen you at your worst—and still love you! Bad hair days, grumpy moods, car breakdowns—they've been there. And the wonder of it all is that, despite your shortcomings, their loyalty remains constant. No matter what you asked of them, you know, deep down, that they'd be there for you.

But did you know you have a Friend who is infinitely more loyal than even your closest friend? Someone who will never disappoint you—even when you've hit rock bottom? Someone who actually died in your place, so you could live a life of joy and wholeness?

I bet you already know who I'm talking about: Jesus. He's the one who "sticks closer than a brother." He not only loves you in spite of your faults, He loves you with your flaws. He doesn't expect perfection from you; He knows you intimately enough to realize that's impossible. Yet your very humanness—your fragility—is what He holds most dearly in His gentle hands. He's the kind shepherd who's left the rest of His flock to come search for you. And He'll never stop searching, no matter how hard you try to hide.

So when you think of that list of close friends, put Jesus at the very top. He's the best, most loyal friend you could ever have.

Best regards,

*Pat Myers*

*Each time before you intercede,
be quiet first, and worship God
in His glory. Think of what He can
do, and how He delights to hear the
prayers of His redeemed
people. Think of your place
and privilege in Christ, and
expect great things!*

Andrew Murray

# WHERE GOD WANTS ME TO BE

Alison Simpson

I'd earned my bachelor's degree in journalism—no doubt about that. I had worked hard, pulled all-nighters, spent time studying instead of goofing off with friends. I had definitely earned that valuable piece of paper. But did I have a plan? Did I know for sure what I wanted to do next? The answer was a resounding "No!" No job waited for me. I didn't even have a single contact in my chosen profession. I had a degree. That was it. The rest was up to me, and I had no idea what to do next.

Finally, I took a job working in a church. It provided me with some work experience to show myself dependable and gave me a steady income while I searched for jobs. I scoured newspapers from places in the country where I thought I'd like to go. I queried for freelance writing opportunities but quickly discovered that I just didn't have a whole lot to write about yet. I even considered going overseas to South Africa to work for a magazine and was hired to do it if I could come up with the money to get there and get started. *What do I do, God?* was my constant prayer.

I seriously thought about the magazine opportunity, and any other person in my position would have been thrilled with an exciting job in a faraway place. But I wasn't sure about moving to South Africa. I wanted to take the job, but deep down, I knew it was the wrong decision. I just didn't know why. So I continued to seek God's direction. I prayed, I studied my Bible, and

I consulted with spiritual mentors whom I trusted, including my pastor.

One day he walked into the office and handed me a book written by a pastor-friend of his about how to know God's will. The book was helpful, but it was my pastor's inscription in the front of the book that rang in my spirit: "Sometimes the Lord's intention in making you wait is to hold you close to Him."

I read those words over and over again. I realized that the future wasn't about my plans. It was about my relationship with God. What was the most important thing to me: God or my plans? Was I looking to God for guidance, or was it to get His approval and rubber-stamp my own plans?

I declined the job in South Africa and stayed at the church until I landed a position at a college working for the public relations director. I delved into graphic design and writing on a freelance basis, giving me the opportunity to put aspects of my education to good use. Then God brought a wonderful man into my life, and I discovered that being a wife and mother was also part of His plan for me.

Where I am now is where God wants me to be. My focus is not on what road to choose next; it's on how I can show my love for God and serve Him where I am today. Maybe I didn't know exactly what I wanted to do, but I definitely knew how I wanted to feel—happy, successful, and fulfilled. God has granted me all that and more. Every day is a journey, and I look forward with excitement to what He has in store for me next.[11] ✒★

# PASTOR, AUTHOR, TEACHER, AND BIBLE TRANSLATOR EUGENE PETERSON

If you had walked into the local butcher shop in a small Montana town in the late 1930s or early 1940s, and noticed the young boy polishing the meat display case or grinding hamburger, you probably would not have suspected that this unassuming young man would one day accomplish something that only one other pastor since the nineteenth century has attempted—a new paraphrase of the Holy Bible. And yet, Eugene Peterson did that and much, much more.

If you had an opportunity to engage the young boy in conversation, you would probably be convinced that he had no idea of the impact his life would have either. He couldn't have known that God would use the plain talk he heard each day from the townsfolk who came into his father's shop to create a homespun version of the Bible that would make the Scriptures come alive for millions of readers. And yet, that's exactly what happened.

Eugene Peterson simply followed the path God had laid out for him. He was faithful with his studies at Seattle Pacific University and New York Theological Seminary. He became a pastor and, along with his wife, Jan, served faithfully for many years, never dreaming of what God still had in store for him in the future. Eventually, it occurred to him that it should be less difficult to understand what is written in God's Word. Since much of the New Testament is in the form of letters to various groups of Christians, it seemed obvious that the original language was far less daunting. The readers of those letters had had little or no trouble understanding what was being said to them. Unfortunately, that ease was lost in the translation from Greek to English. A divinely motivated idea was beginning to form.

Peterson began to play around with the New Testament book of Galatians. Then, calling on the plain talk he grew up with, he attempted to translate a chapter into a more user-friendly form. He paused to imagine how it would have sounded to the Galatian Christians as they read the letters for the first time. The result fascinated him, and he continued on.

Eventually, an editor saw Peterson's work and approached him about translating the entire Bible in this down-home fashion. The project seemed overwhelming at first, but he and his wife prayed. And then, slowly, cautiously, even awkwardly at first, he began to tackle the project. It took twelve years to finish the full translation. Bible scholars monitored his progress along the way to make sure the version was doctrinally sound. Upon completion they dubbed it a vigorous scriptural interpretation for the ordinary person.

This amazing version of the Bible is called *The Message*. It has sold millions of copies, providing an easy, understandable translation of God's Word for young people, those who are reading the Bible for the first time, and even studied Bible readers who find it delightfully refreshing. Because he was faithful to do what God asked him to do at every stage of his life, he became God's instrument to bring something of great value to the world.

It's in Christ that we find out who we are and what we are living for. Long before we first heard of Christ and got our hopes up, he had his eye on us, had designs on us for glorious living, part of the overall purpose he is working out in everything and everyone.

Ephesians 1:11–12 The Message

I delight to do your will, O my God;
your law is within my heart.
Psalm 40:8 NRSV

Conform no longer to the pattern of this present world, but *be transformed by the renewal of your minds.* Then you will be able to discern the will of God, and to know what is good, acceptable, and perfect.

Hebrews 12:2 REB

The great Maker of the will
is alive to carry out
His own intentions.

Charles Spurgeon

God's thoughts, His will, His love, His judgments are all man's home. To think His thoughts, to choose His will, to love His loves, to judge His judgments, and thus to know that He is in us, **is to be at home.**

George MacDonald

God moves in mysterious ways
His wonders to perform;
He plants His footsteps in the sea
And rides upon the storm.

William Cowper

*God is working His purpose out*

*as year succeeds to year.*

*God is working His purpose out*

*and the time is drawing near;*

*Nearer and nearer draws the time,*

*The time that shall surely be,*

*When the earth shall be filled with the glory of God*

*As the waters cover the sea.*

Arthur Campbell Ainger

## The will of God—
## Nothing more. Nothing less.

Author Unknown

# BLOOM WHERE YOU'RE PLANTED

Taprina Milburn

I absolutely love the big city. Everything about the hustle and bustle of urban America—the elbow-to-elbow crowds, the smell of hot dogs cooking in the vendors' carts, taxis sounding their horns, and a Starbucks on every corner.

The seemingly endless opportunities of a big city pulled at me as a college student.

My journalism degree would take me to all the exciting places I wanted to experience, I believed. Maybe I'd have a much sought-after position working for a large daily newspaper covering politics, crime, or even Wall Street. The city would become my city.

I had dreams, and believe me, I wasn't shy about letting God in on those plans.

The president of the Christian university I attended delivered a speech near the end of my senior year and told the students in the crowd, "Bloom where God plants you." I'd heard variations of that charge many times before, but I wrote it in my notebook that morning.

You see, by then I knew I wasn't leaving my small town after graduation. I had since married. My husband had an established career in the town where we lived and where I was finishing up my degree.

God had brought my husband to me, there is no doubt, but

I felt let down. Wasn't God listening to me when I let Him in on my plans? I held regret in my heart that I wouldn't live out my dream of working and living in a large city.

Sometimes regret will prevent blooming.

I landed a job as a reporter in a rural community that neighbors my town. Instead of riding the subway to cover an important political meeting, one of my first assignments was driving my car across a field to take a picture of a farmer and his prize-winning cantaloupe. I've indeed reported on politics, sitting in on town council meetings that went long into the night. And the closest assignments I've had to the nation's financial district were articles about a school bond issue and a comparison piece on the rising cost of cable television.

Not so glamorous, I'll admit.

There was a part of me that felt that if I could only convince my husband to leave our town, I'd have him sold on my big city dream too. That's when my real life and real career would begin. But my efforts led to nowhere. As my husband bloomed and thrived in our town, I chose to remain dormant. He seemed to know something that I didn't.

When you live as if you're headed somewhere else, someplace better than where you are, you don't drop roots. Nor do you relax. Like a shy, nervous kid, you sort of hang back in the shadows and don't risk getting attached to people or places. This isn't the way to live life.

I'm grateful for my husband's steady example, not to mention stubbornness, because along the way I began to love where I was and saw the blessings in the work I was doing right in my own town. I believe the transition had a lot to do with my learning to listen to God's plan for my life rather than acting like a petulant child demanding that He listen to me instead.

Years after that first newspaper job, I bought a brightly colored, whimsical poster that says, "Bloom Where You Are Planted." It hangs on my office wall today and reminds me of what I would have missed if I'd left our town.

God didn't have plans for me to live and work in a big city. Instead He has encouraged me to take root and bloom in a community where I have endless opportunities to listen to and write about the lives of people who sit next to me in church on Sunday or who lead my children in after-school activities (people who don't have a two-hour commute to and from work).

I've since written articles about teen rodeo queens, parents of handicapped children, volunteer firemen, and high school valedictorians, to name only a few. My life is richer for having heard others' stories of faith and struggles, as well as tales of their hopes and dreams—some achieved, but many redirected by God's guiding hand.[12] ✐*

How simple it is to see that all the worry in the world cannot control the future. How simple it is to see that we can only be happy now and that there will never be a time when it is not now.

Gerald Jampolsky

# MISSIONARIES NATHANIEL AND RACHEL SAINT

Nathaniel Saint loved to fly. He took flying lessons in high school, and then used his skills to serve his country during World War II. Following combat, he enrolled in Wheaton College, but the call of the air and the call of Christ were stronger than his desire for a degree. He joined the Mission Aviation Fellowship, and in 1948, he and his wife, Marjorie, went to work in Ecuador, establishing an airbase at an abandoned oil exploration camp. From that simple post, they supplied local missionaries with medicines, mail, and other necessities.

In 1950, their son Steve was born in Ecuador. By the time Steve could walk, he'd go out to the bank of dirt that separated his house from the sand and gravel airstrip and watch his dad take off into the jungle. Then he'd wait for his father to return. Even as a small boy, Steve seemed to sense the dangers inherent in his father's mission.

In September of 1955, three teammates, Jim Elliot, Ed McCully, and Peter Fleming, joined Nate in his effort to reach the Waodani tribe (or Auca settlement) he had found deep in the jungles while searching in the air. Roger Youderian joined them a short time later. Nate knew the tribe was isolated from the modern world, but more importantly, he knew they didn't know about Jesus and His saving power. The group devised a slow, methodological plan to reach out to the tribe in friendship. First, Nate and the team lowered gifts, including machetes and clothing to the Waodani in a bucket tied to the plane. The tribe showed excitement about receiving the gifts, and soon gave gifts of their own. After three months of this give-and-take, the missionaries decided it was time to meet the people on the ground.

On January 3, 1956, they set up camp four miles from the Waodani settlement, using a portion of a riverside beach as a landing strip. The initial personal contact was encouraging—deceptively so. Five days later, the entire team was killed on the beach when armed Waodani met them with thrusting spears and swinging machetes. When the news of the massacre reached base, Steve's mother had the impossible task of telling her son his father would never return home again.

Steve's Aunt Rachel was undeterred and unfazed by the murder of her little brother and the other members of the faithful group of missionaries. She continued to live among the Waodani, teaching them about the trail of Waengongi (God) and the saving love of Itota, His only Son. In fact, by 1964, most of the Waodani had become Christians.

From the time of his father's death, Steve had witnessed his aunt's work among the tribe and was convinced of the authenticity and genuine nature of their faith. One amazing day, there in the river at the place where his father had died, Kimo and Syawi, two of the warriors who had participated in the murders, baptized Steve. Following the example set by his father, mother, and aunt, it never occurred to the fourteen-year-old boy to hate them.

Soon after, Steve returned to America and didn't return to Ecuador until 1994 for the funeral of his beloved Aunt Rachael, who had remained among the Waodani all her life.

By reaching out to a dangerous group of people who didn't know Jesus, Nate Saint paid the ultimate price—his life. But through this and subsequent efforts, the Waodani tribe became followers of Christ. By loving his enemy, Nate Saint taught his son and multitudes of others that there is no price too steep to pay in order to reach those who need the redeeming love of Christ. 🔥

It is not by seeking more fertile regions where toil is lighter—happier circumstances free from difficult complications and troublesome people—but by bringing the **high courage of a devout soul, clear in principles and aim,** to bear upon what is given to us, that we **brighten our inward light, lead something of a true life, and introduce the kingdom of heaven into the midst of our earthly day.** If we cannot work out the will of God where God has placed us, then why has He placed us there?

James H. Thom

My Dear Child,

Your future is in your hands. I've placed it there, and given you the right to choose for yourself the path you will take. If you choose to surrender your will to Mine, I will walk with you every step of the way. I can guarantee that there will be obstacles along the way—difficulties, troubles—but you will never have to face them alone.

What you will do is fulfill the highest purpose for your life—the purpose for which I created you. Your gifts and talents will harmonize with the work at hand, and you will know once and for all that you are—as My servant David said—wonderfully and fearfully made.

Submitting your will to Mine will be adventure of the highest order. Within its bounds, you will find peace, joy, and fulfillment. Even if it includes prison and death as it has for many of My children, you will find My will will take you higher than any earthly accomplishment.

Best of all, you will have the assurance that your life will not be wasted. You will make a difference in the lives of others, for that's the essence of My will—the good of others. When you walk within My will, you become My hands and feet, My heart and tongue, an extension of My purposes on the earth. You will be an instrument of My love to those around you. When you channel My love, My peace, My joy for others, you can't help but soak up a generous portion of it for yourself.

And one more thing—when your future passes from this life to the next, you will find yourself rewarded beyond your wildest dreams for a life well lived. Your future is in your hands. How will you invest it?

*Your loving heavenly Father*

Dear Friend:

When I was in fifth grade I had the privilege of being in Mrs. Francis's class. My older brother raved about her when he heard she would be my teacher. He, along with the rest of the school, loved her ... thought she was the best teacher ever. She was fun, she was smart, and she was always one step ahead of her students. No one could get anything past her, but everyone still loved her and thought she was the coolest teacher in the school.

The memory of Mrs. Francis that I cherish the most (other than our class making Christmas cookies at her house one Saturday morning) was when I was struggling with long division. I hated long division, and I was *awful* at it. I'm not exaggerating about this—math in general was way over my head. So when I encountered long division for the first time, I was filled with trepidation. And sure enough, my homework assignments revealed to Mrs. Francis that I was most definitely in need of help.

One afternoon after class, Mrs. Francis told me she was putting a note to my parents in my backpack. At first I was horrified. But then she explained that she wanted to help me, and she wanted permission to keep me after class. I reluctantly presented the note to my mom, and she agreed that from now on, I'd spend two days a week after school, trying to master long division with Mrs. Francis.

And my fears were correct ... it was frustrating and hard. I remember sitting in the front row of desks staring at the blackboard while she showed me how to work problems, and I felt clueless. Then she had me up at the blackboard, asking me to try, affirming my answers when they were right, and tenderly correcting them when they were wrong. Somehow, faced with a challenge I felt for sure I'd never master, she made me feel like I was smart. She helped me see that I could get this, with perseverance, patience, and a positive attitude.

Not only did she teach me long division, but she also taught me that it was worth it to her to help me. *Why*, I wondered? She could have sent a note home to my parents, saying, "Alison is not grasping long division. Please work with her on this." But she didn't pass the buck. She decided that this was a perfect opportunity to help me see what I could do, and she knew she could help make it happen for me. She took me on as her responsibility because she cared enough about me not only as a student, but also as a person.

Challenges are not opportunities for failure; they're invitations to grow. I learned that best when I was standing at the blackboard with Mrs. Francis. As hard as long division seemed to me, she taught me that it's possible for me to face my fear and then move on to bigger and better challenges. It's all part of being the best kind of me that I can be. Smaller challenges lead to bigger challenges, but the concept is the same: Patience, a positive attitude, and perseverance are three "must-haves" in your toolbox for life. If you've got those things ready and available to you, you can tackle just about anything that comes your way in life.

When I graduated from high school, I moved away and lost touch with Mrs. Francis. But she was definitely my favorite teacher because she cared—not just with her words, but with her actions and her investment in my life. It reminds me of the old adage that children learn how to live, not from our words alone, but from the way we live our lives.

As you seek God's will for your life, I challenge you to begin by making investments that really make a difference in the lives of others. Nothing would be more pleasing to your heavenly Father. And as you take on challenges that seem fierce, remember to offer all your challenges to God so He can reveal His strength in your weaknesses.

You never know, you might even find yourself in the privileged position of being a "Mrs. Francis" to someone else, and watching that beautiful transformation—fear turned into confidence and strength.[13]

Sincerely,

*Alison Simpson*

# PREPARED TO CHANGE THE WORLD

Sharon Gibson

"I don't want to live the American dream, Mom," my son announced to me one afternoon as we discussed his after-graduation plans. "I know I could stay in the U.S., get a good job, have a nice home and a car, but that is not what is in my heart."

I looked at him in disbelief, fearing what was coming next.

Alex had worked hard to obtain his degree, and his achievements were miraculous considering what he had had to overcome.

"I want to go back to the slums to help my brothers and sisters escape the abuse and poverty I left in Brazil," he continued.

Eight years ago, my husband and I had adopted him from an orphanage in Brazil where he had escaped the living hell of a slum there. His mother had severely abused Alex, and he ran away from his home to an orphanage in a nearby neighborhood.

He settled in with us, finished high school, and attended a local university. He returned to Brazil on a summer business internship and located his biological family. He discovered he had seven brothers and sisters, five of them who were born after he left.

Now he wanted to return to Brazil again. I shifted my position as we sat on the living room couch. I frowned. "Dad and I sacrificed for you to be able to have a better life. We did not have in mind for you to return to the slums of Brazil!" I drew a deep breath and sighed, "Brazil is a very long way from here, and I don't really want to be that far from you."

"Mom, I feel God has put this in my heart," he insisted. "My brothers and sisters need me. There are no opportunities for poor kids in Brazil."

I chewed on the end of my glasses as I considered his statements. Finally, I replied, "Who am I to stand in the way of God? If God has put that in your heart to do, then go for it."

His green eyes lit up as he looked at me and smiled. "Thanks, Mom, for understanding."

After graduation, he remained steadfast in his desire to return to Brazil. While his classmates got jobs in their chosen fields and pursued their careers, he set out to fulfill his dream.

That fall my husband and I accompanied Alex to Brazil to meet his brothers and sisters. While we were there, Alex visited with his sister and learned the abuse and neglect of the kids had escalated from two years ago.

Alex was filled with righteous anger, "That's it! I am going to the judge this week to file to have the children taken away from her."

Later that week, my husband, Alex, and I piled in a taxicab to head for the courthouse. I clung to the backseat as the driver hit as many potholes as he missed. I questioned whether or not we were doing the right thing. As if reading my thoughts, Alex said, "Mom, on the phone the social worker said they had been looking for several months for someone to care for these kids."

As I looked at him, I heard the Lord say, "I am just looking for someone to take a stand for these kids." A quote came to mind, "All it takes for evil to prevail is for good men to do nothing." I knew then we had to support our son in his unusual choice regardless of where this journey took us.

Alex obtained temporary custody and decided to stay in Brazil until he could get the permanent guardianship of Michelle, fourteen; Ingrid, nine; Michael, eight; and then bring them to the U.S. Together, they moved into a small two-room house.

In the midst of the intensity of the court fight in Brazil with the mother and the challenge of caring for the children, I called him on the phone. He confided in me, "This is more difficult than I thought. I really miss you, Dad, the U.S., and my friends. I realize one thing; love is about sacrifice. When I wonder if I made the right choice, I look at the kids now compared to when I first got them and I see God's purpose for them and for me. It's worth it."

God calls each of us to change the world. We think an education is a guarantee of the "good life." Maybe we need to think of an education as preparation to change the world.

While for some it may not be as extreme as Alex's sacrifice, it is in our best interest to yield our plans, gifts, and talents to God. Only God knows the paths that will guide us to our destiny, meet the needs of others, and satisfy the desires of our heart.[14]

HELLO FUTURE!

*All heaven is waiting to help those who will discover the will of God and do it.*

J. Robert Ashcrost

You and I may be called over and over again to walk into our own "rivers" of obedience. We may be called to do what we don't understand and what others will not understand. I don't know what river the Lord is asking you to step into, but I do know this: **He is worthy of your complete trust because His will for you is good and perfect whether you feel like it is or not—because He is good!**

Shelly Esser

Dear Friend:

Do you know where all the water that supplies the springs, and fountains, and rills, and rivers of the world comes from? It comes from the ocean in a sort of steam or vapor. The vapor rises, forms clouds, and when the clouds are full, they empty themselves in the form of rain. The rain supplies all the springs and fountains.

The ocean, then, is the grand reservoir from which all the water in the world is obtained. There is more water in the ocean than in all the rest of the world put together; and there is no water in the world but what comes from the ocean. What the ocean is to the world in regard to the supply of water, God is to the world in regard to happiness, from which all the fountains, or sources of happiness, are supplied. All the real happiness which any of God's creatures experience comes from Him. There is more happiness in God than in all the rest of the world or of the universe put together.

Now, seeing this is true, you may well say, "What a wonder it is that all people do not come to God in order to enjoy Him and be happy!" It is a wonder. But the reason for it is that people do not know or believe that there is so much happiness in God. They need someone to show them. They need someone to teach them how to find their enjoyment and happiness in God. And this is what Jesus is able and willing to do for us.

In Matthew 11:29, Jesus says: "Learn from Me." And if we do learn from Him, He will make us very happy. He said on one occasion, "Everyone who drinks this water will be thirsty again, but whoever drinks the water I give him will never thirst. Indeed, the water I give him will become in him a spring of water welling up to eternal life" (John 4:13–14). Those whom Jesus teaches to enjoy God are the happiest people alive. They have more happiness in this life than any other people. And their happiness here cannot compare to the happiness prepared for them in the life to come.

Surely, friend, these are the most valuable lessons you can ever learn. Nobody in the world can teach them to you but Jesus. Answer His invitation to come and learn from Him. If you want to know God, learn from Jesus. If you want to love God, learn of Jesus. If you want to serve God, learn of Jesus. And if you want to enjoy God, learn of Jesus.

Jesus is the best of all teachers, and the knowledge which He gives is the best of all knowledge. The apostle Paul was a very learned man. He had been taught by some of the greatest teachers of his day. But when Paul became a Christian and began to learn of Jesus, he thought the knowledge that He gives to be so excellent that all the other knowledge he had gained was good for nothing in comparison with it. And Paul was right. The knowledge of Christ Jesus our Lord is just as excellent for you as it was for him.

Begin at once to learn from Jesus, and He will make you wise unto salvation. Remember, my dear friend, this is the message of Jesus to you. He says to each one, "Learn from Me."[15]

Sincerely in Jesus,

*Rev. Newton*

If you keep watch over your hearts, and **listen for the voice of God** and learn of Him, in one short hour you can learn more from Him than you can learn from man in a thousand years.

Johann Tauler

# HIS WILL BE DONE

*"His will be done," we say with sighs and trembling,*
*Expecting trial, bitter loss and tears;*
*And then how doth He answer us with blessings*
*In sweet rebuking of our faithless fears.*

*God's will is peace and plenty and the power*
*To be and have the best that He can give,*
*A mind to serve Him and a heart to love Him,*
*The faith to die with, and the strength to live.*

*It means for us all good, all grace, all glory,*
*His kingdom coming and on earth begun.*
*Why should we fear to say: "His will—His righteous,*
*His tender, loving, joyous will—be done?"*

Lucy M. Waelty

*The future is not something we enter. The future is something we create.*

Leonard I. Sweet

# DON'T DIE UNTIL YOU'RE DEAD

The importance of
serving God all of your days,
diligently following
the call of God,
and never giving up!

# YOUR FUTURE IS NOW

The interesting thing about the future is that it stretches out before you, past the restrictions of this life into the endless halls of eternity. For those who place their future in God's hands, there will always be a tomorrow; there will always be hope and a new sunrise preparing to light up the horizon.

That means that no matter how often or how extensively you may fail to achieve your goals, there will be an endless number of tomorrows to try again. Your future will always be ahead of you. What a gift! You will be able to serve God and diligently follow His call all of your days not only here on earth but also in life everlasting.

When you look at your future from that perspective, it makes perfect sense to keep striding forward, pushing disappointments aside, replacing antiquated dreams with new ones, and refusing to give up. It lends itself to flexibility and renewed strength. You literally have all the time in the universe to become all God has planned for you to be.

Apply that principle to the pages ahead. Look at each page in the light of eternity. You may find your enthusiasm is soon over-the-top. What a wonderful privilege it is to love God, serve God, and carry out His will—forever!

This poem was President Abraham Lincoln's favorite. He first heard it sung at a Sunday school convention in Washington in 1864. So impressed was he with the message that he stood and asked to hear it a second time. He kept a copy of the words and often referred to it. Though the words used are from a bygone era, its practical, affirming message is one every person headed out to make his way in the world should hear.

## YOUR MISSION

*If you cannot on the ocean sail among the swiftest fleet*

*Rocking on the highest billows, laughing at the storms you meet,*

*You can stand among the sailors anchored yet within the bay,*

*You can lend a hand to help them as they launch their boats away.*

*If you are too weak to journey up the mountain, steep and high,*

*You can stand within the valley while the multitudes go by.*

*You can chant in happy measure as they slowly pass along—*

*Though they may forget the singer, they will not forget the song.*

*If you have not gold and silver ever ready at command;*
*If you cannot toward the needy reach an ever-helping hand,*
*You can comfort the afflicted. O'er the erring you can weep;*
*With the Savior's true disciples, you a tireless watch may keep.*

*If you cannot in the harvest garner up the richest sheaves,*
*Many a grain, both ripe and golden, of the careless reaper leaves;*
*Go and glean among the briers growing rank against the wall*
*For it may be that their shadow hides the heaviest wheat of all.*

*If you cannot in the conflict prove yourself a soldier true.*
*If where fire and smoke are thickest there's no work for you to do.*
*When the battlefield is silent, you can go with careful tread—*
*You can bear away the wounded. You can cover up the dead.*

*Do not stand idly waiting for some greater work to do;*
*Fortune is a lazy goddess—she will never come to you.*
*Go and toil in any vineyard; do not fear to do or dare—*
*If you want a field of labor you can find it anywhere.*

Mrs. Ellen Gates

# RESOLVED

1. Resolved, to live with all my might while I do live.

2. Resolved, never to lose one moment of time, to improve it in the most profitable way I possibly can.

3. Resolved, never to do anything which I should despise or think meanly of in another.

4. Resolved, never to do anything out of revenge.

5. Resolved, never to do anything which I should be afraid to do if it were the last hour of my life.

Jonathan Edwards

HELLO FUTURE!

# THANK GOD EVERY MORNING

Thank God every morning when you get up that you have something to do that day which must be done, whether you like it or not. Being forced to work, and forced to do your best will breed in you patience and self-control, diligence and strength of will, cheerfulness and content—one hundred virtues that the idle never know.

Charles Kingsley

## Ed Sullivan's Hall of Fame

The great Ed Sullivan was hired by CBS in 1948 to do a weekly Sunday night TV variety show. *The Ed Sullivan Show* was broadcast from CBS Studio 50 on Broadway in New York City, which in 1967 was renamed the Ed Sullivan Theater and is now the home of *The Late Show with David Letterman.*

Sullivan was responsible for introducing many of the greatest acts of the twentieth century to television viewers, including Elvis Presley, Johnny Cash, and the Beatles. In the following essay, he profiles some of the most courageous and tenacious performers of his acquaintance. They simply would not give up and went on to achieve their dreams and live their lives to the fullest.

# ON THE SUBJECT OF COURAGE

Ed Sullivan

To hear Connie Boswell sing, clear, cool notes pouring out of that deep auditorium, you'd hardly think that she was the type of girl who is entitled to all the medals that they pin on individuals for heroism in action. Yet there are few performers who can match the Boswell record of courage. She is one of the few persons living who has had to whip paralysis twice.

The dread disease first manifested itself in New Orleans when she was three years old, brought on when Connie fell off a speeding kid's wagon. She couldn't speak or move a muscle for months. Just when she was returning to normal health, the Boswell Sisters were playing a date at Topeka, Kansas. Connie decided to play a joke on sisters Martha and "Vet" by disappearing from the hotel room. She thought the ground was only a foot below the window. But she fell ten feet to the concrete floor of a basement well. Both legs were paralyzed by the fall.

She's recovered the partial use of her limbs, but has to sing from a wheelchair. The point is that she kept on singing, refused to be counted out, and she's won headline ratings.

Herbert Marshall, after the world war, was left with one leg. By every standard of reckoning Marshall could have enjoyed the prestige of a hero, rested on his laurels. He decided that there was no reason he couldn't go on with his acting career. Doctors advised against it; theatrical producers were dubious. Marshall refused to let them douse his enthusiasm. Today he's one of the top performers in the world.

There is no nicer person in Hollywood. He, who had the right to become bitter, became cheerier than all the rest and more charming. Two years ago, we brought out The Harvest Moon Dance Champions to make a picture. The plan was to get in at the fairly inconvenient hour of 7 a.m. We wanted a movie star to meet the kids at the airport, to give them the thrill of a real movie star welcome. At 7 a.m., Marshall was at the airport, and he made those two youngsters feel that they were the most important persons in the world. In my book, he fits into the Legion of Valor.

Because of its very nature, blindness is a body blow to a professional performer. Managers don't want to engage a performer so afflicted because of the fear that the audience will be depressed by the performer's misfortune. Alec Templeton, however, refused to take the count on his knees. There is only one stipulation in Templeton's act: He is not to be introduced as a blind pianist, and there is to be no reference in advertising or the press to his affliction. He is one of the great acts of show business, a piano virtuoso with a sense of humor so keen that he leaves audiences holding their sides. You've heard performers boast that they "rolled 'em in the aisles." Templeton actually does it.

Nelson Eddy's courage is more responsible for his enormous success than that of any single actor. Lacking the funds to take lessons, he decided that he'd learn to sing in the only way that was open to him. He bought phonograph records of the great operatic baritones, studied their technique, and sang aloud while the records played, to learn where his voice was lacking. His career was handed to him on a platter, but it was not a silver platter.

There have been many sensational dancers in vaudeville. One

of the greatest is Peg Leg Bates, a Carolina boy. I think a train ran over him. Peg Leg, hopping to school one day, fell in love with a girl in the class. His rival was the baseball captain, and the one-legged boy, sick at heart because he couldn't show off his prowess on the baseball diamond like his rival, decided he'd triumph over his handicap. He did. Today he is a show-stopper of vaudeville and night-clubs. His introductory song is a warning to the audience not to give him any sympathy; that he wants to be judged strictly on the merit of his dancing. He performs steps that two-legged dancers can't match.

Raoul Walsh's career as an actor was cut short on a motor trip through Arizona, when a rabbit, frightened by the headlights, leaped through the windshield. The flying glass cost Raoul an eye. He could have folded up. Walsh instead became one of the top film directors of the business.

Lionel Barrymore, for the last two years, has been compelled to use crutches as an aid to walking. You can assume that at times the veteran has suffered physical agony and that he often thought to himself that he had earned the right to rest. His career was not an insignificant career; he could retire and still remain an important memory. Barrymore, instead of quitting, insisted that he'd continue acting. *You Can't Take It with You* found him on the screen, on crutches. *On Borrowed Time* found him turning in a magnificent performance, in a wheelchair. In the prize ring, they call that sort of fortitude "moxie."[16] ⚡★

If you can find a path with no obstacles, it probably doesn't lead anywhere.

Frank A. Clark

A professional is someone who can do his best work when he doesn't feel like it.

Alistair Cooke

**Fall seven times, stand up eight.**

Japanese Proverb

**Obstacles cannot crush me.** Every obstacle yields to stern resolve. **He who is fixed to a star does not change his mind.**

Leonardo da Vinci

Most of our obstacles would melt away if, instead of cowering before them, we should make up our minds to walk boldly through them.
Orison Swet Marden

*[God] will keep you strong to the end, so that you will be blameless on the day of our Lord Jesus Christ.*

1 Corinthians 1:8

**HELLO FUTURE!**

*We are hard pressed on every side, but not crushed;* **perplexed, but not in despair;** *persecuted, but not abandoned;* **struck down, but not destroyed.**

2 Corinthians 4:8–9

*You need to persevere so that when you have done the will of God, you will receive what he has promised.*

Hebrews 10:36

History has demonstrated that the most notable winners usually encountered heartbreaking obstacles before they triumphed. They won because they refused to become discouraged by their defeats.

B. C. Forbes

**Be of good cheer.** Do not think of today's failures, but of the success that may come tomorrow. You have set yourselves a difficult task, but **you will succeed if you persevere;** and you will find joy in overcoming obstacles.

Helen Keller

*Let us not be weary in well doing:*
*for in due season we shall reap,*
*if we faint not.*

Galatians 6:9 KJV

HELLO FUTURE!

## TWELVE REASONS TO SERVE GOD

As you continue to follow the call of God on your life and serve Him faithfully, you may look around you at times and wonder about those who have no concern for God or His purposes. A fair number of them seem to be prospering, happy, and making a place for themselves in the world. They are serving gods of self-interest, money, status, power. It's tempting to look at their lives and question your choice to put your future in God's hands.

The seventeenth-century English clergyman Richard Baxter was known as an effective writer and teacher. During his life, he wrote more than 200 books on the Christian faith. His books, on a number of topics, provided practical advice and enduring values. Encourage yourself with these advantages to serving God:

1. **When you seek to serve God first, you have only one to please rather than multitudes.** If you know you have pleased Him, you know you need worry about no other.

2. **God will never place unreasonable demands on you.** He will not require perfection, nor will He expect you to carry an unhealthy workload.

3. **God will always understand your case** when you bring it before Him, because He is perfectly wise and good.

4. **God will not ask you to do things that are dishonest** or in opposition to your conscience, because He is perfectly holy.

5. **God is impartial and just and treats each person in His service fairly.** He is not swayed by those who would promote themselves at the expense of others.

6. **God rightly judges your circumstances and the reasons for your actions,** because He is intimately acquainted with your heart.

7. **God doesn't waste your time and efforts with contradictions or false starts.** He is perfectly settled on His purposes and direction.

8. **God is perfectly constant and unchangeable.** He is not pleased with one thing today and something different tomorrow. Nor does He favor one person for a time and then discard that person for another.

9. **God is merciful.** As your heavenly Father, He is displeased only with those things that He knows will defile or hurt you. He will not ask you for sacrifices to support His ego.

10. **God is gentle, though just, when He must correct you,** always intending only to build you up and keep you on the right path.

11. **God is not subject to the passions of pride, lust for power, and other** tendencies that blind men's minds and carry them to injustice.

12. **God is not moved by gossip, false accusers, or misinformation.** He knows all.

**Our true worth** does not consist in what human beings think of us. What we really are is what God knows us to be.

John Berchmans

We don't follow him in order to be loved; *we are loved so we follow him.*

Neil Anderson

As long as I see anything to be done for God, life is worth having: but O how vain and unworthy it is to live for any lower end!

David Brainerd's Journal

HELLO FUTURE!

# MISSIONARY DAVID BRAINERD

No one would have blamed him if he'd never left the house. After all, David Brainerd was frail, sickly, tubercular, and to make things worse, he suffered from bouts of depression. But this extraordinary man did not choose to view life from behind a glass window. The call of God was burning in his chest, and he could not say no.

Brainerd's passion was to preach the gospel of Christ to the American Indians. His first journey took him to the forks of the Delaware River; his mission, a ferocious tribe that controlled the area. Before entering the Indian camp, Brainerd stopped to pray. As he knelt there on the ground, he had no idea that he was being watched. Closing his eyes, he silently prayed for the souls of the men and women he was about to encounter. The Indians watched as a rattlesnake appeared next to him, lifted its head to strike inches from his face, and then slithered back into the underbrush. Brainerd never noticed, but the warriors sent out to kill him were amazed and gave him a prophet's welcome.

This incident was just one of many divine interventions that followed David Brainerd as he courageously pursued God's call.

Brainerd's secret weapon was prayer, and he went nowhere without it. So intensely did he plead on behalf of the Indians that he would be covered with sweat and unable to walk straight when his prayers were concluded. Despite his weakened condition, he often fasted as well. He was determined to accomplish God's will for his life.

His prayers were answered and his hard work and sacrifice rewarded as the men and women he so diligently pursued opened their hearts to him and his God. Entire camps were converted. In his diary, Brainerd states: "I know of no assembly of Christians where there seems to be so much of the presence of God, where brotherly love so much prevails."

David Brainerd's life was short. He died of tuberculosis at only twenty-nine years of age. In addition to his work with the Indians, his journal has provided motivation for many to become missionaries, preachers, evangelists, and intercessors. He is considered to be a pioneer of modern missionary work.

## A Passage from David Brainerd's Journal

Nov. 28. In my evening devotion I enjoyed precious discoveries of God, and was unspeakably refreshed with that passage, Hebrews 12:22–24. My soul longed to be conformed to God in all things.—A day or two after I enjoyed much of the light of God's countenance, most of the day; and my soul rested in God.

*We know that in all things God works*
*for the good of those who love him,*
*who have been called*
*according to his purpose.*
Romans 8:28

The only true happiness comes
from **squandering ourselves**
for a purpose.

John Mason Brown

Success is neither fame, wealth,
nor power; rather it is seeking,
knowing, loving, and obeying
God. If you seek, you will
know; if you know, you
will love; if you love,
you will obey.

Charles Malik

Dear Friend:

A questionnaire is, generally speaking, either a nuisance or a bore. But once in a while one comes along that inspires helpful thinking. At such times the interrogated blesses his examiner. That is what I felt one morning recently when I was asked to answer the following:

1.  What is the most valuable lesson life has taught you?

2.  What advice could you give a young person that would help him or her remain balanced in the most difficult experiences in life?

Adolescence is the most difficult period of life, because it seems like every defeat seems final. When you've lived a little longer, you will learn life's first, most valuable lesson—nothing is final.

Disraeli wrote: "Things adjust themselves, more or less badly." Not a very consoling thought put that way. It is just as true that things often turn out well. More often still, actions have no results—they don't amount to anything. After a few weeks or a few months, the situation that seemed at the time to have no possible solution ceases to be anything but a faint memory, a confused picture, a regret.

The man or woman who has lived through the experience of an unendurable present transformed into a blurred past has more power to face affliction, "A terrible power" you might say. "A power made up of indifference and skepticism. Rather than that, just leave me alone with my pain."

But you would be mistaken. Men and women who have reached maturity have not become indifferent. If even in love they know the passion is fleeting, that very thought makes the experience more acute, more ardent. "Nothing is sadder than a second love," Goethe said, "But a third comes and soothes the other two."

I speak here not only of personal problems and private sorrows. In political life it is especially true that long-faced prophets of misfortune unsettle inexperienced young people. Now here again a longer life teaches that events straighten themselves out by time and circumstance. And a wise old Italian diplomat used to say to the young men who surrounded him, "Don't ever say, 'This is very serious.' For sixty years I have been hearing that things are very serious."

As a matter of fact, how can a human situation possibly be otherwise than serious? It is very serious to be a man, to live, to carry on. And yet it is also true that, as the Italian minister suggested, life is very simple, very beautiful; and that it has been going on now for a great many years.

Those are just words, some will think. When you're hurting, the abstract idea of future relief gives little comfort. But life itself shows us the way to more active relief. We learn that we can cut loose from its most painful moments. Flee the place of grief, and the ache will heal. Put some distance between you and the one who has wounded you, and little by little unhappy memories fade. Better still, escape is possible—even without moving from the spot—through the enjoyment of reading, music, or some other form of creation. The function of art in life is to substitute the serene and selfless contemplation of beauty for futile and painful concentration upon one's pain.

Life's second lesson—at least for me—is that few people are

wholly evil. In your first contacts with strangers, you have known only the tenderness of the family circle. You may be frightened by the cruelty, selfishness, and jealousy you see at every turn. Your pessimism is not entirely unfounded: humanity can be appallingly base. But as you come to know people better you will find that they are also capable of kindliness, of enduring tenderness, of great heroism. Then you will begin to realize that what is really fear of life is shielding itself behind the armor of crime.

"What is the most valuable lesson life has taught me?" It is to have a passionate belief in human nature, in spite of her crimes, in spite of her madness.

We come now to the second question, "What advice would you give me that would help me keep my balance in the most difficult experiences of my life?"

That's a question for a book, not for an essay. I think I should begin by insisting on the necessity for discipline. It is not good to be ceaselessly seeking the whys and wherefores of everything. For a life to be happy, it must be based on fixed principles. I would almost say that it is of little importance what those principles are so long as they are solid, steady, and that we accept them without compromise. I am not speaking here of doctrinal creeds. "That," says the poet Byron, "is an affair between a man and his Maker." I am speaking of self-imposed action that builds on a solid base, living by strict discipline. The discipline of a religious life, the discipline of work, of every kind of sport—those are all sane and wholesome, provided they are wholeheartedly believed in.

Another condition that contributes to mental and moral balance seems to me to be unity in the plan, continuity in the pattern. You will undoubtedly be tempted by every possibility and the possibilities are infinite. Limiting yourself to a choice may seem constricting. You want to have every kind of friend; to take every possible journey; to embrace all learning; to embark upon every kind of career. But one of life's conditions is that you must limit yourself; you have to choose. Then and only then can you live deeply and steadily.

These I think would be my answers if I were to answer.[17]

Best wishes,

*André Maurois*

When you look at the world in a narrow way, how narrow it seems! When you look at it in a mean way, how mean it is! When you look at it selfishly, how selfish it is! But when you look at it in a broad, generous, friendly spirit, what wonderful people you find in it.

Horace Rutledge

# WAITING FOR MY DREAM JOB

Therese Stenzel

With visions of designer suits and a corner office, the first job I landed after paying thousands of dollars for a college degree was … a waitress at a restaurant. Actually, I had a brief career as an Admissions Counselor at my college, but when budget cuts came, I went.

Undeterred, I knew I served a big God. He was probably just testing me, so I pressed on. Three months later, I started at a retail shop. Although the work was much easier than waitressing, the pay was awful, and it was humiliating to admit this was all I could find. I kept praying that God would bring a dream job, but nothing changed.

Determined to make things happen, I moved up to a receptionist at a busy medical clinic. By now, my visions of a satisfying career had grown dim. The people I worked beside didn't even have degrees. I'd hear from other college friends who worked in their fields of study—teaching, marketing, health care—and I was answering calls from people with hemorrhoids. *Hello? God, are You there?* Why wasn't He answering my pleas, especially since I was trying so hard?

The clinic I worked for was under severe financial strain, so when the other full-time receptionist quit, they didn't replace her. This left me answering twice the calls and making the same meager wage. I spoke with the administrator and told her this was too much pressure. Many of these calls were from people having heart attacks, women in labor, but she said she didn't have the authority to add personnel.

At this time, I lived in my first apartment with a girlfriend who attended graduate school and lived on a generous trust fund. I, on the other hand, was impoverished, and when my car broke down things only got worse. One day, as I faced a phone system that looked like a lit-up Christmas tree, I snapped. The phone calls, the financial pressure, the overwhelming feeling that God did not care, fell with a bang. Choking back tears, I gathered up my things and walked out of the office. I was a complete failure.

Once inside my silent apartment, I slipped to the floor, partially because I needed to pray and partially because my knees shook so badly I could no longer stand. Would I ever get hired in this town again? As I sobbed out a prayer, a scripture floated through my mind ... "My grace is sufficient for you, for my power is made perfect in weakness."

The second half of that verse flooded my being, and I prayed it aloud, "I will boast all the more gladly about my weaknesses, so that Christ's power may rest on me" (2 Corinthians 12:9).

Right then I laid down all my plans for career, glory, finances, and position. I surrendered my future to Him and told the Lord if He wanted me to work at menial jobs the rest of my life, then so be it. It was more important that I rest in His strength than land the career of my choice.

The next morning, I dressed for work with butterflies slugging it out in my stomach. I appeared before the administrator with my hands folded in front of me. "I am so sorry."

She pursed her lips. "Uh-huh. I had to answer the phones for you all day." She suddenly reached out and grabbed my hands. "I had no idea how much stress you were under. I went to the primary doctor and got him to agree to hire another receptionist."

My head shot up. *Do I sense a little Divine intervention here?* I returned to my desk undaunted by the ringing phones. God was already working on my behalf.

I continued right where I was for six months in total peace. I still worked for peanuts, in a ho-hum position that didn't require a degree, but I had given my career to the Lord, and as I rested in Him, I found there were many facets of my job I enjoyed.

About six months afterward, I saw a position in the paper. I called, and a week later I landed a job as an Admissions Counselor for a trade school where I would achieve all my career goals, including the corner office. But God had so much more in store. There I was able to witness and minister to the students freely, use my degree in communications, and earn a college grad's salary.

A year and a half out of college, I would have considered myself a complete failure, but God had to bring me where I needed to be—on my knees. And when I learned to lean on His strength, He brought about my dream job. [18]   ✸

# WILMA RUDOLPH

Few people would argue that the most popular person at the 1960 Olympics in Rome was Wilma Rudolph, a shy twenty-year-old who was overwhelmed by the crowds that lined the streets shouting, "Vil-ma! Vil-ma!" Even to think that Wilma Rudolph ever made it to Rome was astonishing.

Born the twentieth of twenty-two children to a tobacco plant worker in Tennessee, Wilma found life as a poor Southern black girl was not enough of a challenge. She also had a multitude of childhood illnesses, including pneumonia, scarlet fever, and polio. Her left leg was paralyzed when she was four years old. Wilma later said, "The doctors told me I would never walk, but my mother told me I would, so I believed my mother." Wilma's mother made countless sacrifices to get Wilma the medical treatment she needed, and for two years, family members took turns massaging her leg four times daily. By age six, Wilma could walk with a brace, and soon after, she graduated to an orthopedic high-top shoe. At age eleven she was able to walk unaided, and at thirteen she tried out for the school's basketball team. At fifteen she was All-State.

Wilma always considered running to be pure enjoyment. Her ability on the track—undefeated in three years of competition— resulted in her breaking several state high school records. She tried out for the United States Olympic team, and when she made it, local merchants banded together to give her new clothes and luggage for her first trip by airplane to Australia. She brought home a bronze medal for her part in the 4 x 100-meter relay, and that same year she enrolled at Tennessee State University to run full-time for the

Tigerbelles. Illness and injury struck again, and for two years, Wilma missed most of her track dates. She was determined, however, to make the 1960 Olympics. Even though she had the flu during the trials, she set a world record in the 200 meters and was part of a relay team that won both 100- and 200-meter relays.

Once in Rome, Wilma won her first race, the 100-meter dash, and set a world record. Her second gold was in the 200-meter run. The 400-meter race was more difficult. A mistake was made as the baton was passed to Wilma, and the poor pass allowed the German team to move into first place. Wilma ran with long graceful strides and overtook her German opponent and crossed the finish line a full three yards in the lead. Her run electrified the crowd, and overnight she was heralded around the world as the fastest woman in history.

Olympic victories brought invitations to speak around the world, a thought that scared her far more than any track competition. She rose to the challenge, however, and whenever possible, she used her fame to help advance the cause of civil rights.

After being named the most outstanding female athlete in the world, Wilma retired from running. She generously signed her last pair of track shoes and gave them to a boy who asked for an autograph. She then pursued a career as a second-grade teacher and high-school track coach.

Wilma Rudolph is a profile in courage. She could have let her disabilities define her future. Her determination to be all that she could be has established her as a role model for millions of young women.

*A great deal of talent is lost in this world for want of a little courage.*

Sydney Smith

**All our dreams can come true**, *if we have the courage to pursue them.*

Walt Disney

Let no one nor anything stand between you and the difficult task. Let nothing deny you this rich chance to gain strength by adversity, **confidence by mastery, success by deserving it.** Do it better each time. Do it better than anyone else can do it.

Harlow H. Curtice

*I do not ask to walk smooth paths*
*Nor bear an easy load,*
*I pray for strength and fortitude*
*To climb the rock-strewn road.*
*Give me such courage I can scale*
*The hardest peaks alone,*
*And transform every stumbling block*
*Into a stepping-stone.*

Gail Brook Burket

# A PRACTICAL REMEDY FOR FEAR

Linda Myers-Sowell

Do you have fears—those aching obstacles that hold you back and keep you from becoming all that you can be? Victory may be more accessible than you think. Try doing what you're afraid to do! It's simple; it's practical; it works. I know because I tried it.

Up through high school I was a very timid person. I would rather have taken an F than to have to stand up in front of the class and give an oral report. My mother would have me stand in front of a mirror and practice my reports out loud. At home in front of the mirror I could give the report without looking at my notes. But when I went back into the classroom, I would clam up in fear, and the room would get blurry. Pronouncing the simplest words was a struggle. I would say the report so fast that sometimes teachers would stop me and ask me to slow down, or even worse, ask me to start over.

One year I was required to give an oral report or I would receive an F not just on the report but also on my report card for that quarter. I always enjoyed writing the reports and usually received a very good grade on the writing portion. We were assigned to write a fictional story taken from historical fact. I wrote about Christopher Columbus and received an A for the writing portion. But when the day came to read my report to the class, I choked.

The teacher called my name. "Linda, it is your turn to give

your oral report." He went on to tell the class, "Linda has written an excellent example of a fictional story based on history. Please listen carefully, and you will understand the assignment better."

I should have been filled with confidence after that introduction. Instead, I felt like I was frozen in my seat. When the teacher asked me again to come up in front of the class, I just shook my head no. After school I told the teacher about my fear and accepted an F on my report card. The teacher suggested I take a public-speaking class, but I couldn't imagine being forced week after week to stand up in front of other students to give a speech.

Through my teenage years, I did my best to avoid uncomfortable situations. I longed for the chance to be in a school play, but my fears kept me from the auditions. Instead, I volunteered for the makeup crew. When my friends talked about running for a school office, I always volunteered to write their campaign speeches or make their posters. But my fears kept me from considering myself a candidate.

A year after high school, I ran into one of my former teachers. He asked me what I was doing since graduation. I explained that I was attending college and majoring in English. Then he asked if I had overcome my fear of speaking in public.

"I haven't been required to do that yet this year," I told him.

"Everyone needs to learn to be in front of people, even for just a short period of time" he told me. "It comes with practice, Linda. Have you thought about taking a public speaking class?"

As I continued going to college at night, one of my classes was Assertiveness Training. The instructor helped us to examine ourselves to find what kept us from overcoming our fears. We watched a biographical movie about a woman who had overcome many things in her past to become successful. She had a great fear of heights.

Gradually the woman in the film worked at getting to the top of tall buildings to look down and flew in airplanes until she began to conquer her fears. The final goal she set for herself was to parachute out of an airplane. She screamed for several seconds as she fell toward the earth. She had managed to do the thing she feared most—but she wasn't finished tackling her fears. Her parachute drifted downward until she landed on a lake. It was a planned landing, and a boat quickly came to pick her up. But just before it arrived, she turned toward the camera and told the audience that she was also afraid of water and could not swim.

I found myself strangely inspired by the woman's actions. *If she could overcome her fears by challenging herself in this way, why can't I?*

I began to think of how I could push myself to go beyond what I had perceived were my limits. Meeting people and carrying on conversations were difficult for me. I read books about successful people and found that most people have to learn this art in order to initiate conversations. Studying topics of conversation became fun. Rehearsing in my mind what I would say seemed silly at first, but it also became a habit. Over time, my fear of new people and new surroundings began to diminish.

Finally, I enrolled in a public-speaking class. Each week we were assigned a different topic to talk about for five minutes. I saw what I should have known all along: everyone in the class had knees that were shaking and voices quivering. During the first few speeches I gave I thought I might pass out. My whole body and voice were shaking. After a few weeks, I began to volunteer to give my speech first. That way I could relax the rest of the class time and pay more attention to everyone else's speech. At the end of the semester, I received an A. But in order to be sure I was free, I registered for another semester of public speaking.

Now I'm able to stand up and give a talk anytime I am asked. My only regret is that I waited so long to confront my fear and conquer it—simply by doing what I feared most![19] ✈★

*Courage faces fear and
thereby masters it.*

Martin Luther King Jr.

## Do the thing you fear and the death of fear is certain.

Ralph Waldo Emerson

Having thus chosen our course, let us **renew our trust in God** and **go forward without fear.**
Abraham Lincoln

Courage is not the absence of fear; it is the making of *action in spite of fear,* the moving against the resistance engendered by fear into the unknown and into the future.

M. Scott Peck

# LIVING AND LEARNING

Mary A. Hake

*How would I fit in? Would I be accepted? Could I keep up with the demands?* These were not the jitters of an acned adolescent about to launch out on her own, but the musings of an over-forty mother ready to enter the scary world of college. With many students the ages of my own children and some teachers even younger than I, I wondered how to relate. *Would I be able to meet my expectations? Just what were my expectations anyway?*

When I married the love of my life twenty days before my nineteenth birthday, I held on to my dream of getting a college education some day. I set this dream aside to embrace the roles of wife and mother, later adding homeschool instructor, among other positions. Once my daughters were both in college, I thought now my time had come to join their ranks as a full-time scholar. Enrolling at the local community college made it official. Although I was excited at the prospect, my insides trembled with trepidation. My husband, Ted, who had gone back to college and completed his degree a few years earlier, encouraged me.

Throughout my years of formal education, I had achieved academically, but I never felt successful socially. The web of my youthful inferiority complex no longer strangled me, but fears still attempted to trip my uncertain steps. In spite of the worries nibbling at my mind, I determined to at least give college a try. Unless I participated in campus life—in and out of the classroom—I would never experience all college had to offer, and my dormant desire would remain unfulfilled. Besides, my tuition and books would be paid for since, with three college students in the family, I qualified for a Pell grant and work study. I knew I should take advantage of such an opportunity.

I had always enjoyed learning and valued education more as I grew older. Life's experiences, including teaching our girls as well as the many books and articles I had read through the years, had provided a more than adequate education up to this point. Light-years of changes had occurred, however, in the twenty-plus years since I had graduated from high school. The hi-tech world of higher education seemed intimidating and, at times, overwhelming to me. For example, I had to know how to use a computer just to access the school library.

My memory had already begun exhibiting signs of deterioration. *Would I be able to understand and retain the necessary information in order to pass the tests? Would my courses have any practical application for me in the everyday world?* My mind overflowed with questions. If I couldn't answer my own questions, how would I ever be able to intelligently respond to an instructor's? I realized that without God's assistance I would never succeed.

The first day of fall term, I hesitatingly entered the unfamiliar surroundings. Everyone I met appeared friendly and helpful. I felt accepted and like I belonged. To my surprise and relief, I discovered my former shyness and lack of confidence had disappeared, replaced by a newfound sense of competence. How invigorating! Now I understand why senior citizens often take classes—it keeps them feeling young and alive.

I found I thrived in the stimulating educational environment. I blossomed like a fertilized flower. Summoning my courage and calling on the Lord's aid, I took on new challenges. I surprised my nonmechanical self by successfully tackling Physical Science and Beginning Chemistry. I overcame claustrophobia to learn to develop photos in the tomb-like darkroom. Perseverance and prayer saw me through times of tears, like when I couldn't grasp a math concept or get the proper results on my lab experiment no matter how much I tried. Unabashed joy at mastering difficult assignments rewarded my efforts and kept me coming back for more. Even being injured in a chain collision on my way home from school one day didn't stop me from completing my courses.

This labor of studying and gaining new skills filled three years with struggles, successes, and much personal growth. Along with my college education, I developed a host of new friendships—from students of all ages to faculty members and administrative personnel. I wrote for the campus newspaper, and gradually overcame my nervousness so I could interview anyone from a security guard to the college president.

After cramming in all I could, I looked forward to receiving my associate's degree at graduation. The college recognized only one student with a special award that year. I went forward in a daze to receive the All USA Academic Team certificate.

God has certainly proven Himself faithful in helping me through this season of scholarly learning, just as He has in every stage of my life. How true Paul's words in Philippians 4:13 ring for me: "I can do all things through Christ who strengthens me" (NKJV). Whether it's passing a tough final, giving a speech, caring for a sick family member, or simply living the Christian life day by day, I have learned to lean on God to succeed. Jesus said, "With God all things are possible" (Matthew 19:26 NKJV). I wonder what I should try next.[20]

*You can do what you want to do,*

*Accomplish what you want to accomplish,*

*Attain any reasonable objective you may have in mind—*

*not all of a sudden,*

*Perhaps not in one swift and sweeping act of*

*achievement—*

*But you can do it gradually,*

*Day by day and play by play,*

*If you want to do it,*

*If you work to do it,*

*Over a sufficiently long period of time.*

William E. Holler

# TAKE TIME

*Take time to think—*
*It is the source of all power.*

*Take time to read—*
*It is the fountain of wisdom.*

*Take time to play—*
*It is the source of perpetual youth.*

*Take time to be aware—*
*It is the opportunity to help others.*

*Take time to love and be loved—*
*It is God's greatest gift.*

*Take time to laugh—*
*It is the music of the soul.*

*Take time to dream—*
*It is what the future is made of.*

*Take time to pray—*
*It is the greatest power of earth.*

*Take time to give—*
*Life is too short to be selfish.*

*Take time to work—*
*It is the price of success.*

*There's an opportune time to do things, a*
*right time for everything on the earth.*

Ecclesiastes 3:1 THE MESSAGE

My Precious Child,

The future is beckoning you. Go forward! Don't hesitate, and don't look back. I will be right by your side, encouraging you, guiding you, providing you with the resources you need to succeed in what I've called you to do.

It won't always be easy. There will be tough times—times when you will question your purpose, times when you will almost faint in the face of what lies ahead, times when you will wonder if you have the strength to accomplish My plan for your life. Those times come to all My children. They are normal human responses. The reality is that you can't fulfill your purpose alone. You won't be able to accomplish the great things I've planned for you alone. You will need My help. That's the way it's supposed to be, the way I designed it. I will never ask you to do anything that we cannot do together.

When you feel used up, discouraged, weak, don't hide from Me or try to disguise your true feelings. Instead, come to Me. Receive your comfort, your consolation, your encouragement, your strength from Me. I will refresh you, renew you, and stand you again on your feet. If need be, I will carry you!

My plan for you, My child, is not designed to defeat you, but to give you a future and a hope. It is a plan to keep us close, a plan to give your life on earth meaning and significance, a plan to give you a part in building My kingdom.

*Your loving heavenly Father*

I know what I'm doing. I have it all planned out—plans to take care of you, not abandon you, plans to give you the future you hope for. When you call on me, when you come and pray to me, I'll listen. When you come looking for me, you'll find me. Yes, when you get serious about finding me and want it more than anything else, I'll make sure **you won't be disappointed.**

Jeremiah 29:11–14 THE MESSAGE

# THE RIGHT JOB FOR ME!

Jean Wensink

In 1982, I graduated from college with a degree in elementary education and was ready to take the classroom by storm. I was praying to land a job by the end of the summer so that I could begin the school year teaching. But where would the Lord lead me?

After sending out one hundred letters and resumes, I received a few calls for interviews. I wasn't too fussy about location or even grade level; I just wanted to begin my career. Each time I interviewed, I would get my hopes up, envisioning where I would start my new life, set up my apartment, and live an adult lifestyle. But after each rejection, I was dejected and wondered if I would ever get a job. I began to question my career choice, planned for a future without teaching, and wondered how God would use me. I was compelled to put my life in God's hands and be willing to go wherever He led me.

I continued to apply for anything that I was qualified for, confident that God would reveal His plan for my life. After all, my future was in His hands. At the end of August, I was called to interview at a small technical college. I would be teaching computers and math to adults. Perhaps this was where I was needed. I was qualified for the job.

As I was waiting to hear their decision, a tiny school district called me to interview the very next day. One of their teachers had unexpectedly broken her contract, and they needed a

**HELLO FUTURE!**

new teacher immediately because school was starting in less than a week. Without even knowing where the district was located, I said of course I could come for the interview and took down directions. Early the next morning, I got dressed in my interviewing outfit, thinking that this was probably my last chance for a job because schools would be starting. I said a prayer and asked for God's leading, safe travels, and, of course, His calming assurance.

The position was everything I had hoped for. I would be teaching first grade at a small rural school. The school was spacious, quaint, and built next to a church. It seemed perfect for me, but would the interviewing team feel the same way? As I drove the ninety minutes home, I prayed that an answer would be revealed. Which job was right for me, the technical college or the elementary position? How would I decide if I had to choose between the two? What if I wasn't offered either job?

I pulled my old car in the driveway, ran into the kitchen, and greeted my mom and dad with a "Hi, I'm home!" Just then the phone rang. It was the school district calling, and they offered me the first grade position. I would start the very next day! I eagerly accepted, hung up the phone, and let out a whoop that was heard throughout the house. I had landed a job!

During my dancing and jumping around, my mom brought in the mail and noticed an important-looking letter addressed to me in the batch. It was from the technical college, offering me the position of adult math and computer teacher. There was quite a difference between the two positions—especially in terms of salary. That evening I wrote a letter to turn down the position teaching adults even though it seemed to be the better of the two offers.

Now, twenty-four years later I am still teaching in the same district. I still love teaching young children and know that it is my calling. Every time I try to spread my wings and try my hand at administration or teaching college, the Lord nudges me back to the classroom. He has His ways of putting people where He wants them in order to do His work. We just have to be open and listen to His voice.[21]

*Success in our calling is the result of a person's love of and belief in the work he or she has undertaken. Earnest and conscientious labor often accomplishes more in the end than brilliant genius.*

Author Unknown

Nothing splendid has ever been achieved except by those who dared believe that something inside them was superior to circumstances.

Bruce Barton

HELLO FUTURE!

The long span of the bridge of your life is supported by countless cables called habits, attitudes, and desires. What you do in life depends upon what you are and what you want. **What you get from life depends upon how much you want it**—how much you are willing to work and plan and cooperate and use your resources. The long span of the bridge of your life is supported by countless cables that you are spinning now, and that is why today is such an important day. Make the cables strong.

L. G. Elliott

*We work day after day, not to finish things, but to make the future better because we will spend the rest of our lives there.*

Charles Kettering

*Greatness, in the last analysis, is largely bravery—courage in escaping from old ideas and old standards, and respectable ways of doing things. This is one of the chief elements in what we vaguely call capacity. If you do not dare differ from your associates and teachers, you will never be great or your life sublime. You may be the happier as a result, or you may be miserable. Each of us is great insofar as we perceive and act on the infinite possibilities which are undiscovered and unrecognized about us.*

James Harvey Robinson

HELLO FUTURE!

Many live in dread of what is coming. Why should we? **The unknown puts adventure into life.** It gives us something to sharpen our souls on. The unexpected around the corner gives a sense of anticipation and surprise. **Thank God for the unknown future.**

E. Stanley Jones

*The best thing about the future is that it comes only one day at a time.*

Abraham Lincoln

*There's a saying I've heard—most people offer it as a lesson for living; that life is divided into three phases: you learn, you earn, then you serve. By that yardstick, you've done your learning, and now it's time to do some earning—to build the career that allows you to give back later.*

J. C. Watts

# Notes

1   Caroline Jalango. www.motivationzone.com. Article Source: www. goalsettingarticles.com. Used by permission of the author.

2   Alison Simpson, Frankfort, Kentucky. *The Beauty of Our Dreams*. Used by permission of the author.

3   Brenna Fay Rhodes, Waco, Texas. *You Can Do This!* Used by permission of the author.

4   Coleen P. Kenny, Glen Allen, Virginia. *The Perfect Place to Start*. Used by permission of the author.

5   Kimberly J. Fish, Longview, Texas. *For the Love of Goats*. Used by permission of the author.

6   Bonnie Compton Hanson, Santa Ana, California. *You Write the Songs*. Used by permission of the author.

7   Deborah Bates Cavitt, Duncanville, Texas. *Avid for Animation*. Used by permission of the author.

8   Lavon Hightower Lewis, Vinita, Oklahoma. *Joseph, the Prince of Egypt*. Used by permission of the author.

9   Elece Hollis, Boynton, Oklahoma. *F Is for Future*. Used by permission of the author.

10  Rev. Richard Newton. *The Gift for God*. Taken from *Rills from the Fountain of Life*, 1889.

11  Alison Simpson, Frankfort, Kentucky. *Where God Wants Me to Be*. Used by permission of the author.

12  Taprina Milburn, Shawnee, Oklahoma. *Bloom Where You're Planted*. Used by permission of the author.

13  Alison Simpson, Frankfort, Kentucky. *Dear Friend*. Used by permission of the author.

14  Sharon Gibson, Siloam Springs, Arkansas. *Prepared to Change the World*. Used by permission of the author.

15  Rev. Richard Newton. *The Gift for God*. Taken from *Rills from the Fountain of Life*, 1889.

16  Ed Sullivan. *On the Subject of Courage.*

17  André Maurois. *Lessons and Advice.*

18  Therese Stenzel, Tulsa, Oklahoma. *Waiting for My Dream Job.* Used by permission of the author.

19  Linda Myers-Sowell, Wichita, Kansas. *A Practical Remedy for Fear.* Used by permission of the author.

20  Mary A. Hake, Crooked River Ranch, Oregon. *Living and Learning.* Used by permission of the author.

21  Jean Wensink, Sheboygan Falls, Wisconsin. *The Right Job for Me!* Used by permission of the author.